Handmade LOVE FROM YOUR KITCHEN & CRAFT ROOM

51

Few things warm hearts like a gift from the kitchen or the craft room. Now, for the first time, the team at *Taste of Home* has combined the best treats, sweets, mixes and must-haves with quick crafts, clever packing ideas and nifty name tags perfect for gift-giving all year long! With **Taste of Home Handmade Food Gifts**, it's never been easier (or more delicious) to show someone how much you care.

Take a look inside and you'll find:

- **112 recipes** that make ideal presents
- Dozens of **creative ideas** for wrapping food gifts
- More than **85 full-color photos**
- **A bonus chapter** of holiday favorites
- Nutrition facts as well as **prep times**

Best of all, these food gifts come from home crafters, cooks and bakers just like you! These are the ideas they turn to when they want to create a gift from the kitchen. In addition, each recipe was tested and approved at the *Taste of Home* Test Kitchen, so you know everything will turn out wonderfully.

From teachers and coaches to neighbors, friends and family, everyone loves a treat from the heart. And with **Handmade Food Gifts** at your side, you'll find just the right surprise for everyone on your list.

26

TASTE OF HOME BOOKS • RDA ENTHUSIAST BRANDS, LLC • MILWAUKEE, WI

Visit us at **tasteofhome.com** for other Taste of Home books and products.
ISBN: 978-1-62145-582-0
LOCC: 2019931313
Component: PR00150440

Deputy Editor: Mark Hagen
Senior Art Director: Raeann Thompson
Designer: Jazmin Delgado
Copy Editors: Chris McLaughlin, Ann Walter

Photographer: Mark Derse
Market Producer/Set Stylist: Stacey Genaw
Food Stylist: Lauren Knoelke

Pictured on front cover:
Crunchy Granola Pretzel Sticks, p. 42

**Pictured on back cover
(clockwise from top left):**
A Cup of Coffee Cake, p. 1; Spiced Almond Brittle, p. 41; Strawberry-Basil Vinegar, p. 57; Orange-Cranberry Nut Bread, p.67; Hot Buttered Cider Mix, p. 28; Chive Biscuit Ornaments, p. 89; Almond Pistachio Baklava, p. 77; Carrot Cake Jam, p. 47

Printed in China.
1 3 5 7 9 10 8 6 4 2

78

57

69

CONTENTS

More ways to connect with us:

Handmade
GIFTS IN A JAR

FAVORITE BREAD & BUTTER PICKLES

I made these pickles while growing up and love them because you can eat them with just about anything. They're fine gifts for giving any time of the year.
—*Linda Weger, Robinson, IL*

· ·

Prep: 45 min. + standing
Process: 10 min./batch
Makes: 11 pints

- 20 cups sliced cucumbers
  (about 12 medium)
- 3 cups sliced onions
  (about 4 medium)
- 1 medium sweet red pepper, sliced
- 1 medium green pepper, sliced
- 3 qt. ice water
- ½ cup canning salt
- 6 cups sugar
- 6 cups white vinegar
- 3 Tbsp. mustard seed
- 3 tsp. celery seed
- 1½ tsp. ground turmeric
- ¼ tsp. plus ⅛ tsp. ground cloves

1. Place cucumbers, onions and peppers in a large bowl. In another large bowl, mix ice water and salt; pour over vegetables. Let stand 3 hours.
2. Rinse vegetables and drain well. Pack vegetables into eleven hot 1-pint jars to within ½ in. of the top.
3. In a Dutch oven, bring sugar, vinegar, mustard seed, celery seed, turmeric and cloves to a boil. Carefully ladle hot liquid over vegetable mixture, leaving ½-in. of headspace. Remove the air bubbles and adjust headspace, if necessary, by adding hot liquid. Wipe rims. Center lids on jars; screw on bands until fingertip tight.
4. Place jars into canner, ensuring that they are completely covered with water. Bring to a boil; process for 10 minutes. Remove jars and cool.

NOTE: The processing time listed is for altitudes of 1,000 feet or less. For altitudes up to 3,000 feet, add 5 minutes; 6,000 feet, add 10 minutes; 8,000 feet, add 15 minutes; 10,000 feet, add 20 minutes.
¼ CUP: 60 cal., 0 fat (0 sat. fat), 0 chol., 645mg sod., 15g carb. (14g sugars, 0 fiber), 0 pro.

SPICY PICKLED GARLIC

Here's a delicious condiment for the garlic lover on your list. You will be pleasantly surprised by the way pickling mellows out the garlic and makes it a tasty topper for sandwiches.
—*Taste of Home Test Kitchen*

· ·

Prep: 20 min.
Process: 10 min.
Makes: 3 half-pints

- 2 qt. water
- 3 cups peeled garlic cloves
- 12 coriander seeds
- 6 whole peppercorns
- 3 dried hot chiles, split
- 3 whole allspice
- 1 bay leaf, torn into three pieces
- 1½ cups white wine vinegar or
  distilled white vinegar
- 1 Tbsp. sugar
- 1½ tsp. canning salt

1. In a large saucepan, bring water to a boil. Add the garlic and boil 1 minute.
2. Meanwhile, divide the coriander, peppercorns, chiles, allspice and bay leaf among three hot half-pint jars. Drain the garlic and pack it into the jars to within ½ in. of the top.
3. In a small saucepan, combine vinegar, sugar and salt. Bring to a boil, stirring constantly. Carefully ladle hot liquid over garlic, leaving ½-in. headspace. Remove air bubbles and adjust the headspace, if necessary, by adding hot mixture. Wipe rims. Center lids on jars; screw on bands until fingertip tight.
4. Carefully place jars into canner with simmering water, ensuring that they are completely covered with water. Bring to a boil; process for 10 minutes. Remove jars and cool.

NOTE: The processing time listed is for altitudes of 1,000 feet or less. For altitudes up to 3,000 feet, add 5 minutes; 6,000 feet, add 10 minutes; 8,000 feet, add 15 minutes; 10,000 feet, add 20 minutes.
1 GARLIC CLOVE: 5 cal., 0 fat (0 sat. fat), 0 chol., 30mg sod., 1g carb. (0 sugars, 0 fiber), 0 pro.

TRIPLE CHOCOLATE COOKIE MIX

Everyone likes a good old-fashioned cookie mix—and this one is especially popular with chocoholics! I like to tie the directions for preparation and baking to the jar with a colorful ribbon.
—*Patricia Swart, Galloway, NJ*

Prep: 30 min.
Bake: 15 min./batch
Makes: 5 dozen

2¼ cups all-purpose flour, divided
1 tsp. baking powder
½ tsp. salt
½ tsp. baking soda
½ cup baking cocoa
1 cup packed brown sugar
½ cup sugar
¾ cup semisweet chocolate chips
¾ cup white baking chips
ADDITIONAL INGREDIENTS
¾ cup butter, melted and cooled
3 large eggs, room temperature
3 tsp. vanilla extract

1. In a small bowl, whisk 1¼ cups flour, baking powder, salt and baking soda. In another bowl, whisk cocoa and remaining flour. In an airtight 5-cup container, layer half of the flour mixture and half of cocoa mixture; repeat. Layer sugars and chips in the order listed. Cover and store in a cool, dry place up to 3 months.
2. To prepare cookies: Preheat oven to 350°. In a large bowl, beat butter, eggs and vanilla until well blended. Add cookie mix; mix well.
3. Drop by tablespoonfuls 2 in. apart onto ungreased baking sheets. Bake until firm, 12-14 minutes. Remove from pans to wire racks to cool. Store cookies in an airtight container.
1 COOKIE: 86 cal., 4g fat (2g sat. fat), 16mg chol., 63 mg sod., 12g carb. (8g sugars, 0 fiber, 1g pro.

GINGERBREAD CAKE MIX

I put this mixture together for gifts, but also for my own use. This way, I can bake up the moist, nicely spiced gingerbread in no time. It's especially handy during the hectic holiday season.
—*Ruth Seitz, Columbus Junction, IA*

. . . .

Prep: 15 min.
Bake: 35 min.
Makes: 9 servings per batch

  6⅔ cups all-purpose flour
  1½ cups sugar
  ¾ cup plus 1 Tbsp. nonfat
    dry milk powder
  ¼ cup baking powder
  1 Tbsp. salt
  2½ tsp. ground cinnamon
  2 tsp. cream of tartar
  1¼ tsp. ground cloves
  1¼ tsp. ground ginger
  1½ cups shortening
ADDITIONAL INGREDIENTS
    (FOR EACH BATCH)
  1 large egg, room temperature
  ½ cup water
  ½ cup molasses

1. In a large bowl, combine the first nine ingredients. Cut in the shortening until mixture resembles coarse crumbs. Store mixture in five airtight pint containers in a cool, dry place for up to 6 months. Yield: 5 batches (10 cups total).

2. To prepare cake: Preheat oven to 350°. Lightly beat egg, water and molasses. Add one jar (2 cups) of cake mix; beat until well blended. Spread into a greased 8-in. square baking pan. Bake until a toothpick inserted in center comes out clean, 35-40 minutes. Cool on a wire rack.

NOTE: Contents of mix may settle during storage. When preparing recipe, spoon mix into the bowl or measuring cup.

1 PIECE: 218 cal., 7g fat (2g sat. fat), 24mg chol., 290mg sod., 35g carb. (19g sugars, 1g fiber), 3g pro.

DIY RAMEN SOUP

This jarred version of ramen soup is a healthier alternative to most commercial varieties. You can customize the veggies if you'd like.
—Michelle Clair, Seattle, WA

Takes: 25 min.
Makes: 2 servings

- 1 pkg. (3 oz.) ramen noodles
- 1 Tbsp. reduced-sodium chicken base
- 1 to 2 tsp. Sriracha Asian hot chili sauce
- 1 tsp. minced fresh gingerroot
- ½ cup shredded carrots
- ½ cup shredded cabbage
- 2 radishes, halved and sliced
- ½ cup sliced fresh shiitake mushrooms
- 1 cup shredded cooked chicken breast
- ¼ cup fresh cilantro leaves
- 1 hard-boiled large egg, halved
- 2 lime wedges
- 4 cups boiling water

1. Cook ramen according to package directions; cool. In each of two 1-qt. wide-mouth canning jars, divide and layer ingredients in the following order: ramen noodles, chicken base, Sriracha, ginger, carrots, cabbage, radishes, mushrooms, chicken and cilantro. Place egg and lime wedge in 4-oz. glass jars or other airtight containers. Place on top of cilantro in 1-qt. jars. Cover and refrigerate mixture until serving.

2. To serve, remove egg and lime. Pour 2 cups boiling water into each 1-qt. glass jar; let stand until warmed through or until chicken base has dissolved. Stir to combine seasonings. Squeeze lime juice over soup and place egg on top.

1 SERVING: 401 cal., 14g fat (6g sat. fat), 153mg chol., 1092mg sod., 35g carb. (4g sugars, 2g fiber), 31g pro.

DELICIOUS CHOCOLATE SAUCE

My sauce mixes up in a matter of minutes! One batch yields so much that I have plenty extra to give out as gifts. Pair the tasty sauce with gourmet cones and colorful toppings to make a complete ice cream shop gift package.
—Dorothy Anderson, Ottawa, KS

Prep: 5 min.
Cook: 10 min. + cooling
Makes: 4 cups

- ½ cup butter, cubed
- 4 oz. unsweetened chocolate, chopped
- 3 cups sugar
- ½ tsp. salt
- 1 can (12 oz.) evaporated milk
- 1 tsp. vanilla extract

1. In a small heavy saucepan, melt butter and chocolate over low heat; stir in sugar and salt. Gradually stir in milk; cook and stir until sugar is dissolved. Remove from heat; stir in vanilla.

2. Serve warm or at room temperature (sauce will thicken upon cooling). Store, covered, in refrigerator.

2 TBSP.: 87 cal., 1g fat (1g sat. fat), 3mg chol., 47mg sod., 20g carb. (20g sugars, 0 fiber), 1g pro.

SPICY BAVARIAN BEER MUSTARD

Here's a gift that has bite! Serve this spicy beer mustard with all kinds of pretzels or as a condiment for bratwurst.
—Taste of Home *Test Kitchen*

. . . .

Prep: 15 min. + chilling
Process: 15 min.
Makes: 7 half-pints

2 cups dark beer
2 cups brown mustard seed
2 cups ground mustard
1½ cups packed brown sugar
1½ cups malt vinegar
½ cup balsamic vinegar
3 tsp. salt
2 tsp. ground allspice
½ tsp. ground cloves
2 tsp. vanilla extract

1. In a small bowl, combine beer and mustard seeds. Cover and refrigerate mixture overnight.
2. Place seed mixture in a blender. Cover and process until chopped and slightly grainy. Transfer to a Dutch oven. Add the ground mustard, brown sugar, vinegars, salt, allspice and cloves. Bring just to a boil. Remove from heat; stir in vanilla.
3. Ladle hot liquid into seven hot half-pint jars, leaving ½-in. headspace. Wipe rims. Center lids on jars; screw on bands until fingertip tight.
4. Place jars into canner with simmering water, ensuring that they are completely covered with water. Bring to a boil; process for 10 minutes. Remove the jars and cool.
NOTE: The processing time listed is for altitudes of 1,000 feet or less. For altitudes up to 3,000 feet, add 5 minutes; 6,000 feet, add 10 minutes; 8,000 feet, add 15 minutes; 10,000 feet, add 20 minutes.
1 TBSP.: 36 cal., 1g fat (0 sat. fat), 0 chol., 65mg sod., 5g carb. (3g sugars, 1g fiber), 1g pro.

SOUTHERN PIMIENTO CHEESE SPREAD

Pimiento cheese is the ultimate southern comfort food. We serve it as a dip for crackers, chips and celery or slather it on burgers and hot dogs.
—*Eileen Balmer, South Bend, IN*

. . . .

Prep: 10 min. + chilling
Makes: 1¼ cups

1½ cups shredded cheddar cheese
1 jar (4 oz.) diced pimientos, drained and finely chopped
⅓ cup mayonnaise
Assorted crackers

Combine the cheese, pimientos and mayonnaise. Refrigerate mixture for at least 1 hour. Serve with crackers.
2 TBSP.: 116 cal., 11g fat (4g sat. fat), 21mg chol., 144mg sod., 1g carb. (0 sugars, 0 fiber), 4g pro.

SPINACH PESTO

Serve this vibrant pesto on pasta, pizza, sandwiches and more. If you don't have fresh oregano on hand, you can omit it.
—*Susan Westerfield, Albuquerque, NM*

Takes: 15 min.
Makes: 2 cups

- 2 cups fresh baby spinach
- 2 cups loosely packed basil leaves
- 1 cup grated Romano cheese
- 2 Tbsp. fresh oregano
- 2 tsp. minced garlic
- ½ tsp. salt
- ½ cup chopped walnuts, toasted
- 1 Tbsp. lemon juice
- 2 tsp. grated lemon zest
- 1 cup olive oil

Place the first six ingredients in a food processor; cover and pulse until chopped. Add the walnuts, lemon juice and zest; cover and process until blended. While processing, gradually add oil in a steady stream. Keep refrigerated.

2 TBSP.: 177 cal., 18g fat (4g sat. fat), 8mg chol., 205mg sod., 1g carb. (0 sugars, 1g fiber), 4g pro.

> **HOMEMADE HELPER**
> Add a jar of this pesto to a pasta dinner basket or simply include a few handwritten recipe cards featuring your family's favorite dishes that call for prepared pesto.

SALTED CASHEW OATMEAL COOKIES

My son absolutely loves cashews, and I loaded my oatmeal cookies with them at Christmas—he loved them! Give the mix to friends, co-workers and teachers for birthdays or holidays; all they have to do is add butter, vanilla and eggs.
—*Richard Hatch, Glen Burnie, MD*

Prep: 20 min.
Bake: 10 min./batch + cooling
Makes: 1 batch (about 4 cups mix)

- 1 cup all-purpose flour
- ¾ tsp. baking soda
- ¾ tsp. ground cinnamon
- ½ cup packed light brown sugar
- ½ cup sugar
- 1⅓ cups old-fashioned oats
- 1 cup salted whole cashews

ADDITIONAL INGREDIENTS
- ⅔ cup butter, softened
- ¾ tsp. vanilla extract
- 1 large egg plus 1 large egg yolk, room temperature

1. Whisk together the flour, baking soda and cinnamon. In a 1-qt. glass jar, layer flour mixture, brown sugar, granulated sugar, oats and cashews in order listed. Cover and store in a cool dry place for up to 3 months.

2. To prepare cookies: Preheat oven to 350°. Beat butter and vanilla extract until light and fluffy. Add egg and yolk until well blended. Add cookie mixture; mix well

3. Drop by tablespoonfuls 1½ in. apart on parchment-lined baking sheets. Bake until lightly browned, 10-12 minutes. Remove from pans to wire racks to cool.

1 COOKIE: 104 cal., 6g fat (3g sat. fat), 19mg chol., 73mg sod., 12g carb. (6g sugars, 1g fiber), 2g pro.

PLUM CONSERVE

This mouthwatering conserve is a heartwarming and versatile gift. It makes a lovely garnish for rolls during holiday feasts, is delicious paired with cheese as an appetizer, and it also delights as an ice cream or pound cake topping for dessert.
—*Ginny Beadle, Spokane, WA*

Prep: 40 min.
Process: 10 min.
Makes: 7 half-pints

- 2 lbs. medium Italian plums, pitted and quartered
- 1½ cups dried cranberries
- ½ cup quartered and thinly sliced mandarin oranges
- ½ cup orange juice
- 3 cups sugar, divided
- 1 pkg. (1¾ oz.) powdered fruit pectin
- 1 cup coarsely chopped walnuts

1. In a Dutch oven, combine the plums, cranberries, oranges, orange juice and 2½ cups sugar. Mix remaining sugar with pectin; set aside. Bring to a full rolling boil over high heat, stirring constantly, until slightly thickened and the plums soften, about 15 minutes. Stir in pectin mixture and walnuts; return to a full rolling boil. Boil and stir 1 minute.
2. Remove from heat. Ladle hot mixture into seven hot half-pint jars, leaving ¼-in. headspace. Remove the air bubbles and adjust headspace, if necessary, by adding hot mixture. Wipe rims. Center lids on jars; screw on bands until fingertip tight.
3. Carefully place jars into the canner with simmering water, ensuring that they are completely covered with water. Bring to a boil; process for 10 minutes. Remove jars and cool.

NOTE: The processing time listed is for altitudes of 1,000 feet or less. Add 1 minute to the processing time for each 1,000 feet of additional altitude.

2 TBSP.: 81 cal., 2g fat (0 sat. fat), 0 chol., 0 sod., 18g carb. (16g sugars, 1g fiber), 0 pro.

SAND ART BROWNIES

A jar of this layered mix produces a yummy batch of fudgy brownies that are dressed up with chocolate chips and M&M's. If you need a quick gift for a neighbor or teacher, this is truly a delicious solution.
—*Joan Hohwald, Lodi, NY*

Prep: 15 min.
Bake: 30 min. + cooling
Makes: 16 servings

- 1 cup plus 2 Tbsp. all-purpose flour
- ½ tsp. salt
- ½ tsp. baking powder
- ⅓ cup baking cocoa
- ⅔ cup sugar
- ⅔ cup packed brown sugar
- ½ cup semisweet chocolate chips
- ½ cup milk chocolate M&M's

ADDITIONAL INGREDIENTS
- 3 large eggs, room temperature
- ⅔ cup vegetable oil
- 1 tsp. vanilla extract

1. Combine flour, salt and baking powder. In a 1-qt. glass container, layer the flour mixture, cocoa, sugar, brown sugar, chocolate chips and M&M's, packing well between each layer. Cover and store in a cool, dry place up to 6 months.
2. To prepare brownies: Preheat oven to 350°. Beat eggs, oil and vanilla. Stir in the brownie mix.
3. Pour into a greased 8-in. square baking dish. Bake until center is set, 26-28 minutes (do not overbake). Cool on a wire rack.

1 SERVING: 256 cal., 13g fat (3g sat. fat), 41mg chol., 106mg sod., 33g carb. (24g sugars, 1g fiber), 3g pro.

BUTTERSCOTCH BROWNIE MIX

Most people have butter, eggs and vanilla on hand, and those ingredients are all friends and family will need to turn this gift mix into a delicious pan of golden butterscotch brownies.
—*Macey Allen, Green Forest, AR*

. . . .

Prep: 15 min.
Bake: 20 min. + cooling
Makes: 2 dozen

- 2 cups all-purpose flour
- 3½ tsp. baking powder
- ¼ tsp. salt
- ¾ cup chopped pecans, toasted
- 1½ cups packed brown sugar
- ½ cup butterscotch chips

ADDITIONAL INGREDIENTS
- ¾ cup butter, cubed
- 2 large eggs, room temperature
- 2 tsp. vanilla extract

1. In a small bowl, mix flour, baking powder and salt. In a 1-qt. glass jar, layer flour mixture, pecans, brown sugar and butterscotch chips in the order listed. Cover and store in a cool, dry place up to 3 months. Yield: 1 batch (about 4 cups brownie mix).

2. To prepare brownies: Preheat oven to 350°. In a large saucepan, heat butter over medium heat until just melted. Remove from heat. Whisk in eggs and vanilla until blended. Gradually add the brownie mix, mixing well. Spread into a greased 13x9-in. baking pan.

3. Bake 20-25 minutes or until a toothpick inserted in center comes out with moist crumbs (do not overbake). Completely cool in pan on a wire rack.

1 BROWNIE: 198 cal., 10g fat (5g sat. fat), 31mg chol., 154mg sod., 25g carb. (17g sugars, 1g fiber), 2g pro.

BANANA-CHIP MUFFIN MIX

Here's a chocolate-dotted version of classic banana bread. Jars of the fun layered mix always go over big with my family during the holidays.
—*Edie DeSpain, Logan, UT*

Prep: 10 min.
Bake: 10 min./batch
Makes: 4 dozen

- 2¼ cups all-purpose flour
- 2 tsp. baking powder
- ½ tsp. salt
- 1 cup packed brown sugar
- 1 cup M&M's minis or miniature semisweet chocolate chips

ADDITIONAL INGREDIENTS
- 1 cup mashed ripe bananas (about 2 large)
- ½ cup butter, melted
- 2 large eggs, room temperature
- ½ tsp. vanilla extract

1. In a small bowl, combine the flour, baking powder and salt. In a 1-qt. glass jar, layer the flour mixture, brown sugar and M&M's. Cover and store in a cool, dry place for up to 3 months. Yield: 1 batch (about 4 cups mix).

2. To prepare muffins: Place muffin mix in a large bowl. Whisk the bananas, butter, eggs and vanilla; stir into dry ingredients just until moistened. Fill 48 greased or paper-lined mini-muffin cups three-fourths full. Bake the muffins at 400° until a toothpick comes out clean, 9-10 minutes. Serve warm.

1 MUFFIN: 87 cal., 3g fat (2g sat. fat), 14mg chol., 60mg sod., 13g carb. (8g sugars, 1g fiber), 1g pro.

TO MAKE REGULAR MUFFINS: Fill greased or paper-lined muffin cups three-fourths full. Bake at 400° until a toothpick comes out clean, 14-16 minutes. Serve warm.

A GIFT FOR THE GREEN THUMB

Giving is always in season, so why not share flower bulbs and gardening fun with a friend?

- Place natural sisal in the bottom of a jar. Roll up a pair of garden gloves with a bit of twine. Fill jar with the gloves and tiny gifts such as seed packets, bulbs and even plant markers. Replace the lid.

- Wrap several strands of raffia around the jar lid and tie a knot, leaving 2-in. ends. Thread one end through the hole of a gift tag with name and message.

- To make a tassel, cut a short piece of raffia and wrap it around the ends of the jar's raffia tie. Knot.

- Embellish the lid by gluing on paper flowers purchased from a craft store.

A CUP OF COFFEE CAKE

This mix is easy, delicious and full of the flavors folks need to get through their day! Instant coffee works fine as a substitute for the brewed, if you like.
—*Deborah Dubord, Fayette, ME*

Prep: 10 min.
Bake: 25 min.
Makes: 1 batch (about 3½ cups mix)

- ½ cup chopped walnuts
- ½ cup semisweet chocolate chips
- 1½ cups all-purpose flour
- ½ tsp. salt
- ½ tsp. baking soda
- 1 cup packed brown sugar

ADDITIONAL INGREDIENTS

- 1 large egg, room temperature
- ½ cup brewed coffee, room temperature
- ½ cup canola oil

1. Place walnuts and chocolate chips in a small plastic bag. Whisk together flour, salt and baking soda. Transfer to a 1-qt. glass jar. Layer with brown sugar and the walnut mixture. Cover and store in a cool dry place up to 3 months.
2. To prepare coffee cake: Preheat oven to 350°. Whisk egg, coffee and canola oil. Add flour and brown sugar mixture; mix until combined. Pour the batter into a greased 8-in. square baking pan. Sprinkle with nuts and chocolate chips. Bake until a toothpick inserted in center comes out clean, 25-30 minutes. Cool on a wire rack.
1 PIECE: 374 cal., 20g fat (3g sat. fat), 21mg chol., 218mg sod., 47g carb. (29g sugars, 2g fiber), 4g pro.

> **HOMEMADE HELPER**
> A little goes a long way, particularly when it comes to dressing up jars for gifts. Notice how the simple scrap of cotton ribbon adds easy flair to the mason jar at left.

HOMEMADE SALSA

You know it's an amazing salsa when your guests hover around the serving plate till it's scraped clean! This version boasts fresh cilantro, cranberries and just a hint of heat from a jalapeno pepper.
—*Shelly Pattison, Lubbock, TX*

Prep: 20 min. + chilling
Makes: 12 servings

- 1 pkg. (12 oz.) fresh or frozen cranberries
- 1 cup sugar
- 6 green onions, chopped
- ½ cup fresh cilantro leaves, chopped
- 1 jalapeno pepper, seeded and finely chopped
- 1 pkg. (8 oz.) cream cheese, softened
  Assorted crackers or tortilla chips

1. Pulse cranberries and sugar in a food processor until coarsely chopped. Stir together with the onions, cilantro and jalapeno. Cover and refrigerate several hours or overnight.
2. To serve, place cream cheese on a serving plate. Drain the salsa; spoon over the cream cheese. Serve with crackers or chips.
NOTE: Wear disposable gloves when cutting hot peppers; the oils can burn skin. Avoid touching your face.
1 SERVING: 146 cal., 7g fat (4g sat. fat), 21mg chol., 71mg sod., 22g carb. (19g sugars, 2g fiber), 1g pro.

CHICAGO-STYLE HOT GIARDINIERA

I've been living in Chicago for the last 12 years and have grown to love the spicy giardiniera served at so many restaurants here. I developed my own version to use at home. We love it on everything from eggs to sandwiches—and even pizza.
—*Andrea Quiroz, Chicago, IL*

. . . .

Prep: 30 min. + chilling
Makes: 8 cups

- 1 small head cauliflower, broken into small florets (about 5 cups)
- 2 celery ribs, chopped
- 1 medium carrot, chopped
- 4 jalapeno peppers, sliced
- 4 serrano peppers, sliced
- ½ cup salt
- 1 cup white vinegar
- 3 garlic cloves, minced
- 2 tsp. dried oregano
- 1 tsp. crushed red pepper flakes
- 1 cup canola oil
- 1 jar (10 oz.) small pimiento-stuffed olives, drained

1. In a large bowl, toss the cauliflower, celery, carrot and peppers with salt. Add cold water to cover. Refrigerate mixture, covered, overnight.

2. Drain vegetables; rinse with cold water and drain again. In a large nonreactive bowl, whisk vinegar, garlic, oregano and pepper flakes. Gradually whisk in oil until blended. Add the olives and the drained vegetables; toss to coat. Refrigerate, covered, overnight to allow the flavors to blend.

3. Transfer mixture to jars. Cover and refrigerate up to 3 weeks.

NOTE: Wear disposable gloves when cutting hot peppers; the oils can burn skin. Avoid touching your face.

¼ **CUP:** 80 cal., 8g fat (1g sat. fat), 0 chol., 174mg sod., 2g carb. (0 sugars, 0 fiber), 0 pro.

GERMAN BEER CHEESE SPREAD

We love the bold flavors tied to our German heritage. Cheddar and beer make a tangy spread to serve with pretzels, pumpernickel, crackers and sausage. Choose your favorite beer because the flavor comes through in the finished recipe.

—Angela Spengler, Niceville, FL

Takes: 15 min.
Makes: 2½ cups

- 1 lb. sharp cheddar cheese, cut into ½-in. cubes
- 1 Tbsp. Worcestershire sauce
- 1½ tsp. prepared mustard
- 1 small garlic clove, minced
- ¼ tsp. salt
- ⅛ tsp. pepper
- ⅔ cup German beer or nonalcoholic beer
  Assorted crackers or vegetables

1. Place cheese in a food processor; pulse until finely chopped, about 1 minute. Add Worcestershire sauce, mustard, garlic, salt and pepper. Gradually add beer while continuing to process until the mixture is smooth and spreadable, processing for about 1½ minutes.
2. Transfer to a serving bowl or gift jars. Refrigerate, covered, up to 1 week. Serve with crackers or vegetables.

2 TBSP.: 95 cal., 8g fat (5g sat. fat), 24mg chol., 187mg sod., 1g carb. (0 sugars, 0 fiber), 6g pro.

> **READER RAVE**
> *"Fantastic and easy dip. It was a huge hit."*
> —LINDAS_WI, TASTEOFHOME.COM

Handmade
MUST-TRY
MIXES

WINTER HERB TEA MIX

This caffeine-free option is a sweet-spicy blend of mint, sage, rosemary, thyme and honey that melts away winter blahs.
—*Sue Gronholz, Beaver Dam, WI*

. . . .

Takes: 10 min.
Makes: 18 servings (9 Tbsp. mix)

- 6 Tbsp. dried mint
- 1 Tbsp. dried sage leaves
- 1 Tbsp. dried rosemary, crushed
- 1 Tbsp. dried thyme

ADDITIONAL INGREDIENTS
(FOR EACH SERVING)
- 1 cup boiling water
- 1 tsp. honey
- 1 lemon wedge

1. In a small airtight container, combine the herbs. Store in a cool, dry place for up to 6 months.
2. To prepare tea: Place 1½ tsp. tea mix in a glass measuring cup. With the end of a wooden spoon handle, crush mixture until aromas are released. Add boiling water. Cover and steep for 10 minutes. Strain tea into a mug, discarding herbs. Stir in honey; serve with lemon.

1 CUP HOT TEA: 27 cal., 0 fat (0 sat. fat), 0 chol., 2mg sod., 7g carb. (6g sugars, 1g fiber), 0 pro.

> **HOMEMADE HELPER**
> While they don't spoil, dried herbs do lose potency over time. For tea with maximum flavor, don't use herbs that are over a year old. Store dried herbs in airtight containers away from heat and light.

GRANOLA STREUSEL CRANBERRY MUFFIN MIX

These delicious muffins are perfect for breakfast. Once the family gets a taste, they're sure to disappear quickly!
—*Karen Moore, Jacksonville, FL*

. . . .

Takes: 30 min.
Makes: 1 dozen

- 2 cups all-purpose flour
- ½ cup nonfat dry milk powder
- ½ cup sugar
- 3 tsp. baking powder
- 1 tsp. pumpkin pie spice
- ½ tsp. salt
- ¾ cup dried cranberries

STREUSEL
- 2 crunchy oat and honey granola bars (0.74 oz. each), finely crushed
- 2 Tbsp. sugar

ADDITIONAL INGREDIENTS
- 1 large egg, lightly beaten, room temperature
- ¾ cup water or 2% milk
- ⅓ cup canola oil
- 2 Tbsp. butter, melted

1. Whisk together first six ingredients. Place in a 1-qt. jar; top with cranberries. In a small plastic bag, combine the streusel ingredients. Add to jar; cover. Store in a cool dry place up to 3 months.
2. To prepare muffins: Preheat oven to 375°. Place muffin mix in a large bowl. In a small bowl, whisk egg, water and canola oil until blended. Add to muffin mix; stir just until moistened. Fill 12 paper or foil-lined muffin cups three-fourths full. Combine streusel with melted butter. Sprinkle evenly over muffin cups.
3. Bake until a toothpick inserted in the center comes out clean, 15-18 minutes. Cool 5 minutes before removing from pan to a wire rack. Serve warm.

1 MUFFIN: 251 cal., 9g fat (2g sat. fat), 21mg chol., 271mg sod., 39g carb. (20g sugars, 1g fiber), 4g pro.

BLUEBERRY MAPLE SUGAR PANCAKE MIX

We use maple sugar made at our farm, Bonhomie Acres, in these pancakes, and then we top them with 100 percent maple syrup, too. The delicious flavor demands nothing less!

—*Katherine Brown, Fredericktown, OH*

. . . .

Prep: 15 min. • **Cook:** 5 min./batch
Makes: 15 pancakes (about 2 cups mix)

- 2 cups all-purpose flour
- 4 tsp. baking powder
- ½ tsp. salt
- ⅓ cup maple sugar
- ⅔ cup dried blueberries

ADDITIONAL INGREDIENTS
- 2 large eggs
- 1⅓ cups 2% milk
- ¼ cup butter, melted

1. Whisk together flour, baking powder and salt. Transfer to a 1-pt. glass jar. Top with maple sugar; cover. Place the dried blueberries in a small plastic bag; attach to jar. Store in a cool dry place or in a freezer up to 3 months.

2. To prepare pancakes: Preheat lightly greased griddle over medium heat. In a small bowl, mix flour mixture and maple sugar. Whisk in eggs, milk and melted butter. Stir in blueberries.

3. Pour batter by scant ¼ cupfuls onto griddle; cook until bubbles on top begin to pop and the bottoms are golden brown. Turn; cook until the second side is golden brown.

3 PANCAKES: 437 cal., 13g fat (7g sat. fat), 104mg chol., 757mg sod., 69g carb. (24g sugars, 3g fiber), 10g pro.

HEARTY PASTA SOUP MIX

Warm up loved ones on frosty winter nights with a gift of this stick-to-the-ribs soup mix. Packed in pretty glass jars, it looks just as good as it tastes! Be sure to include preparation instructions and a list of additional ingredients needed with your gift card.
—Taste of Home *Test Kitchen*

. . . .

Prep: 15 min.
Cook: 1¼ hours
Makes: 14 servings (3½ qt.)

- ½ cup dried split peas
- 2 Tbsp. chicken bouillon granules
- ½ cup dried lentils
- 2 Tbsp. dried minced onion
- 1 tsp. dried basil
- 1 tsp. dried parsley flakes
- 1 envelope savory herb with garlic soup mix or vegetable soup mix
- 2 cups uncooked tricolor spiral pasta

ADDITIONAL INGREDIENTS
- 10 cups water
- 3 cups cubed cooked chicken
- 1 can (28 oz.) diced tomatoes, undrained

1. In a half-pint glass container, layer the first seven ingredients in the order listed; seal tightly. Place the pasta in a 1-pint resealable jar; seal.

2. To prepare the soup: Place water in a Dutch oven; stir in the soup mix. Bring to a boil. Reduce heat; cover and simmer for 45 minutes. Add the chicken, tomatoes and pasta. Cover and simmer mixture until the pasta, peas and lentils are tender, 15-20 minutes longer.

1 CUP SOUP: 173 cal., 3g fat (1g sat. fat), 27mg chol., 613mg sod., 22g carb. (3g sugars, 5g fiber), 15g pro.

> **READER RAVE**
> *"I received this as a gift. I didn't have any chicken on hand, so I used ½ lb. of smoked sausage. It was delicious! I plan to make this as gifts next year."*
> —KTDOZIER, TASTEOFHOME.COM

APPLESAUCE MUFFIN MIX

I adapted a recipe so I could give this homemade muffin mix to our family as gifts. They can make them when they want to—it's like giving a gift twice!
—*Barbara Opperwall, Wyoming, MI*

Takes: 30 min. • **Makes:** 9 muffins

- ½ cup sugar
- 1¼ tsp. baking powder
- 1 tsp. ground cinnamon
- ½ tsp. ground nutmeg
- ¼ tsp. salt
- 1½ cups all-purpose flour, divided
- 2 Tbsp. quick-cooking oats

ADDITIONAL INGREDIENTS
- 1 large egg, lightly beaten, room temperature
- 1 cup unsweetened applesauce
- ½ cup butter, melted
- 1 tsp. vanilla extract
- 1 Tbsp. sugar

1. Combine the first five ingredients. In a 1-pint glass jar, layer ¾ cup of flour, the oats, sugar mixture and the remaining flour. Cover and store in a cool, dry place for up to 6 months.
2. To prepare muffins: Preheat oven to 375°. Combine egg, applesauce, butter and vanilla. Stir in muffin mix just until moistened. Fill greased muffin cups three-fourths full. Sprinkle with sugar. Bake until a toothpick comes out clean, 15-20 minutes. Cool 5 minutes before removing from pan to a wire rack.
1 MUFFIN: 240 cal., 11g fat (7g sat. fat), 51mg chol., 232mg sod., 33g carb. (15g sugars, 1g fiber), 3g pro.

CONFETTI BEAN SOUP MIX

With its colorful variety of beans and delicious flavor, this tempting soup makes a great gift for friends each Christmas.
—*Rebecca Lambert, Staunton, VA*

Prep: 20 min. + standing
Cook: 1 hour 25 min.
Makes: 4 batches/9 servings per batch

- 1 lb. each dried navy beans, great northern beans, red kidney beans, pinto beans and green split peas

SEASONING MIX
- 12 beef bouillon cubes
- ¾ cup dried minced chives
- 4 tsp. dried savory
- 2 tsp. ground cumin
- 2 tsp. coarsely ground pepper
- 4 bay leaves

ADDITIONAL INGREDIENTS (FOR EACH BATCH)
- 12 cups water, divided
- 1 can (14½ oz.) stewed tomatoes, undrained
- 1½ tsp. salt
- ¼ tsp. hot pepper sauce, optional

1. Combine beans and peas; place 3 cups of the mixture in each of four large glass jars. Set aside.
2. In each of four snack-size plastic bags, place three bouillon cubes, 3 Tbsp. chives, 1 tsp. savory, ½ tsp. cumin, ½ tsp. pepper and one bay leaf. Attach a bag to each jar with ribbon or length of twine.
3. To prepare soup: Place the contents of one bag of beans in a Dutch oven; add 7 cups of water. Bring to a boil; boil for 2 minutes. Remove from heat; cover pan and let stand for 1 hour.
4. Drain the beans and discard liquid. Add the remaining 5 cups of water and contents of one seasoning bag. Bring to a boil. Reduce heat; cover and simmer, stirring occasionally, until the beans are tender, about 1 hour.
5. Add tomatoes, salt and, if desired, pepper sauce. Simmer, uncovered, for 20 minutes. Discard bay leaf.
1 CUP SOUP: 230 cal., 1g fat (0 sat. fat), 0 chol., 477mg sod., 43g carb. (6g sugars, 14g fiber), 15g pro.

SPLIT PEA SOUP MIX

My mother sent me this pretty blend along with the recipe. The hearty soup is thick with lentils, barley and peas; chicken is a nice change from the usual ham.
—*Susan Ruckert, Tangent, OR*

. . . .

Prep: 10 min. • **Cook:** 1¼ hours
Makes: 13 batches / 4 servings per batch

- 1 pkg. (16 oz.) dried green split peas
- 1 pkg. (16 oz.) dried yellow split peas
- 1 pkg. (16 oz.) dried lentils, rinsed
- 1 pkg. (16 oz.) medium pearl barley
- 1 pkg. (12 oz.) alphabet pasta
- 1 jar (½ oz.) dried celery flakes
- ½ cup dried parsley flakes

ADDITIONAL INGREDIENTS
(FOR EACH BATCH)

- 4 cups chicken broth
- ¼ tsp. pepper
- 1 cup cubed cooked chicken, optional

1. Combine the first seven ingredients. Transfer to airtight containers, or divide equally among 13 plastic bags. Store in a cool, dry place for up to 1 year.

2. To prepare soup: In a large saucepan, combine 1 cup soup mix with broth, pepper and, if desired, cubed chicken. Bring to a boil. Reduce heat; simmer, covered, until peas and lentils are tender, 1 to 1¼ hours.

1 CUP SOUP: 158 cal., 3g fat (0 sat. fat), 7mg chol., 117mg sod., 26g carb. (0 sugars, 0 fiber), 11g pro. **DIABETIC EXCHANGES:** 1½ starch, 1 lean meat.

CHERRY-ALMOND TEA MIX

Our family enjoys giving homemade gifts for Christmas and other special occasions. Beverage mixes such as this one are especially popular. The soothing tea is a favorite.
—*Andrea Horton, Kelso, WA*

. . . .

Takes: 10 min.
Makes: 40 servings (2½ cups mix)

- 2¼ cups iced tea mix with lemon and sugar
- 2 envelopes (0.13 oz. each) unsweetened cherry Kool-Aid mix
- 2 tsp. almond extract

ADDITIONAL INGREDIENT
(FOR EACH SERVING)

- 1 cup boiling water

1. Place tea mix, Kool-Aid mix and extract in a food processor; pulse until blended. Store in an airtight container in a cool, dry place up to 6 months.

2. To prepare tea: Place 1 Tbsp. tea mix in a mug. Stir in 1 cup boiling water until disolved and blended.

1 CUP TEA: 41 cal., 0 fat (0 sat. fat), 0 chol., 1mg sod., 10g carb. (10g sugars, 0 fiber), 0 pro.

> **HOMEMADE HELPER**
> This tea also makes a great summer refresher—instead of mixing in a mug with boiling water, use cold water. Serve in a tall glass over ice, and you have a perfect hot-weather drink!

• • •

HOT BUTTERED CIDER MIX

Put the butter base for this beverage in a decorative jar and attach a copy of the recipe for a great gift from your kitchen. You can simply omit the brandy for a kid-friendly version.

—Taste of Home *Test Kitchen*

Takes: 10 min.
Makes: 64 servings (2 cups mix)

- 1   cup butter, softened
- 1   cup packed brown sugar
- ½   cup honey
- 1   tsp. ground cinnamon
- ½   tsp. ground cardamom
- ¼   tsp. ground cloves

ADDITIONAL INGREDIENTSS
(FOR EACH SERVING)
- ¾   cup hot apple cider or juice
- 1   oz. apple brandy, optional

1. Beat butter and brown sugar until blended; beat in honey and spices. Transfer to an airtight container. Store in refrigerator up to 2 weeks.
2. To prepare hot cider: Place 1½ tsp. buttered cider mix in a mug. Stir in hot cider and, if desired, brandy.
¾ CUP CIDER: 136 cal., 3g fat (2g sat. fat), 8mg chol., 40mg sod., 28g carb. (25g sugars, 0 fiber), 0 pro.

JAMBALAYA MIX

With your zippy jambalaya mix on hand, friends will find a full-flavored meal is never far away. Shrimp, smoked sausage and a few other easy additions to the nicely seasoned rice mix create a speedy skillet sensation.

—*Sybil Brown, Highland, CA*

Takes: 25 min.
Makes: 3 batches/6 servings per batch

- 3   cups uncooked long grain rice
- 3   Tbsp. dried minced onion
- 3   Tbsp. dried parsley flakes
- 4   tsp. beef bouillon granules
- 1   Tbsp. dried minced chives
- 1   Tbsp. dried celery flakes
- 1½ tsp. pepper
- ¾   tsp. cayenne pepper
- ¾   tsp. garlic powder
- ¾   tsp. dried thyme

ADDITIONAL INGREDIENTS
(FOR EACH BATCH)
- 2   cups water
- ½   cup chopped green pepper
- 1   can (8 oz.) tomato sauce
- 1   lb. smoked sausage, cut into ¼-in. slices
- 1   lb. uncooked shrimp (31-40 per lb.), peeled and deveined

1. Combine the first 10 ingredients. Divide into three equal batches; store in airtight containers in a cool, dry place for up to 6 months.
2. To prepare the jambalaya: In a small saucepan, bring water and green pepper to a boil. Stir in 1 cup jambalaya mix; return to a boil. Reduce heat; cover and simmer until rice is tender, 18-20 minutes.
3. In another saucepan, heat the tomato sauce and sausage. Cook shrimp in boiling water until pink; drain. Stir into sausage mixture. Serve with rice mixture.
1 CUP JAMBALAYA: 423 cal., 21g fat (9g sat. fat), 163mg chol., 1335mg sod., 30g carb. (3g sugars, 1g fiber), 26g pro.

RED LENTIL SOUP MIX

Give your friends the gift of good health. Red lentils are a protein powerhouse and are loaded with folate, iron and fiber. Oh, and this soup tastes amazing, too.
—Taste of Home *Test Kitchen*

Prep: 25 min. • **Cook:** 25 min.
Makes: 4 batches/4 servings per batch

- 2 pkg. (1 lb. each) dried red lentils
- ¼ cup dried minced onion
- 2 Tbsp. dried parsley flakes
- 2 tsp. ground allspice
- 2 tsp. ground cumin
- 2 tsp. ground turmeric
- 1½ tsp. salt
- 1 tsp. garlic powder
- 1 tsp. ground cardamom
- 1 tsp. ground cinnamon
- 1 tsp. pepper
- ½ tsp. ground cloves

ADDITIONAL INGREDIENTS (FOR EACH BATCH)

- 1 medium carrot, finely chopped
- 1 celery rib, finely chopped
- 1 Tbsp. olive oil
- 2 cans (14½ oz. each) vegetable broth

1. Place 1⅓ cups lentils in each of four 12-oz. jelly jars. Combine the next 11 ingredients. Evenly divide onion mixture among small cellophane bags; place sealed bags inside jars, on top of lentils. Store in a cool, dry place up to 6 months.
2. To prepare soup: Rinse lentils and drain. In a large saucepan over medium-high heat, saute carrot and celery in oil until tender. Add lentils, onion mixture and broth. Bring to a boil. Reduce heat; simmer, covered, until lentils are tender, 10-15 minutes.

1 CUP SOUP: 257 cal., 4g fat (1g sat. fat), 0 chol., 1067mg sod., 42g carb. (4g sugars, 7g fiber), 14g pro.

HOMEMADE RANCH DRESSING & DIP MIX

Keep this versatile blend on hand to whip up a delicious veggie dip or salad dressing on a moment's notice. The jar of mix also makes a great gift—just remember to attach a copy of the recipe.
—*Joan Hallford, North Richland Hills, TX*

Prep: 10 min. + chilling
Makes: 4 batches dressing or 2 of dip

- 2 Tbsp. dried parsley flakes
- 1 Tbsp. garlic powder
- 1 Tbsp. dried minced chives
- 2 tsp. lemon-pepper seasoning
- 1½ tsp. dried oregano
- 1½ tsp. dried tarragon
- 1 tsp. salt

ADDITIONAL INGREDIENTS FOR SALAD DRESSING (FOR EACH BATCH)

- ½ cup mayonnaise
- ½ cup buttermilk

ADDITIONAL INGREDIENTS FOR DIP (FOR EACH BATCH)

- 1 cup mayonnaise
- 1 cup sour cream

1. Mix the seasonings until well blended. Transfer to an airtight container. Store in a cool, dry place for up to 1 year. Shake to redistribute seasonings before using.
2. To prepare salad dressing: Whisk together mayonnaise, buttermilk and 1 Tbsp. mix. Refrigerate, covered, for at least 1 hour before serving.
3. To prepare dip: Mix mayonnaise, sour cream and 2 Tbsp. mix until blended. Refrigerate, covered, at least 2 hours before serving.

2 TBSP. DRESSING: 108 cal., 11g fat (2g sat. fat), 6mg chol., 198mg sod., 1g carb. (1g sugars, 0 fiber), 1g pro.

HERB MIX FOR DIPPING OIL

Combine a blend of herbs to create this mouthwatering mix. Plumping the herbs in water before stirring them into olive oil enhances the flavor.

—Taste of Home *Test Kitchen*

. . . .

Takes: 5 min.
Makes: 3 batches (½ cup per batch)

- 1 **Tbsp. dried minced garlic**
- 1 **Tbsp. dried rosemary, crushed**
- 1 **Tbsp. dried oregano**
- 2 **tsp. dried basil**
- 1 **tsp. crushed red pepper flakes**
- ½ **tsp. salt**
- ½ **tsp. coarsely ground pepper**

ADDITIONAL INGREDIENTS
(FOR EACH BATCH)

- 1 **Tbsp. water**
- ½ **cup olive oil**
- 1 **French bread baguette (10½ oz.)**

1. In a small bowl, combine the first seven ingredients. Store in an airtight container in a cool, dry place for up to 6 months.

2. To prepare the dipping oil: In a small microwave-safe bowl, combine 4 tsp. of the herb mix with water. Microwave, uncovered, on high for 10-15 seconds. Drain excess water. Transfer herbs to a shallow serving plate; add oil and stir. Serve with bread.

1 TBSP.: 122 cal., 14g fat (2g sat. fat), 0 chol., 50mg sod., 1g carb. (0 sugars, 0 fiber), 0 pro.

READER RAVE
"I made this for friends—they told me it was better than what they had in expensive Italian restaurants."
—ROBIN, TASTEOFHOME.COM

• • •

APPLE-CINNAMON OATMEAL MIX

Oatmeal is a breakfast staple at our house. We used to buy the oatmeal mixes, but we think our homemade version is better! Feel free to substitute raisins or other dried fruit for the apples.

—*Lynne Van Wagenen, Salt Lake City, UT*

Takes: 5 min. • **Makes:** 16 servings

- 6 **cups quick-cooking oats**
- 1⅓ **cups nonfat dry milk powder**
- 1 **cup dried apples, diced**
- ¼ **cup sugar**
- ¼ **cup packed brown sugar**
- 1 **Tbsp. ground cinnamon**
- 1 **tsp. salt**
- ¼ **tsp. ground cloves**

ADDITIONAL INGREDIENT (FOR EACH SERVING)

- ½ **cup water**

1. In a large bowl, combine the first eight ingredients. Store in an airtight container in a cool, dry place for up to 6 months.
2. To prepare oatmeal: Shake mix well. In a small saucepan, bring water to a boil; slowly stir in ½ cup of the mix. Cook and stir over medium heat for 1 minute. Remove from the heat. Cover and let stand for 1 minute or until the oatmeal reaches desired consistency.

½ CUP OATMEAL: 171 cal., 2g fat (0 sat. fat), 1mg chol., 185mg sod., 34g carb. (13g sugars, 4g fiber), 6g pro. **DIABETIC EXCHANGES:** 2 starch.

PRETTY PACKAGING IDEAS

Often the most priceless gifts are your very own homemade treats—even better when you present them in seasonal tins or a pretty package. Looking for some suggestions?

- Layer cookies or candies in a wide-mouth canning jar, cover the lid with fabric and screw on the band. (You may want to include the recipe!)

- Wash empty glass or tin food containers with lids, and decorate the outside with wrapping paper or contact paper. Attach a bow to the lid.

- Wrap sweets in plastic wrap, set a bow on top and tuck the package inside a coffee mug or teacup.

- Craft stores sell papier-mache boxes with holiday themes. In a star-shaped box lined with waxed paper, stack some star-shaped sugar cookies.

- Look for decorative tins, plates and candy dishes throughout the year at stores, rummage sales and after-Christmas sales. Keep them on hand for last-minute gifts.

CHIPPY CHOCOLATE COOKIE MIX

I've had this simple recipe for a long time, and I got the idea of layering the mix after seeing similar gift mixes in stores. I have yet to meet the person who doesn't rave over the cookies. You can use M&M's in place of the peanut butter chips.
—*Francine Wingate,*
New Smyrna Beach, FL

Prep: 10 min. • **Bake:** 15 min./batch
Makes: 2 dozen

- 1 **pkg. chocolate cake mix (regular size)**
- 1 **cup peanut butter chips**

ADDITIONAL INGREDIENTS

- ½ **cup canola oil**
- 2 **large eggs, room temperature**

1. In a 1-qt. glass container, layer half of the cake mix, peanut butter chips and remaining cake mix. Cover and store in a cool, dry place up to 6 months.
2. To prepare cookies: Preheat oven to 350°. Combine cookie mix, oil and eggs. Drop by rounded tablespoonfuls 2 in. apart onto ungreased baking sheets. Bake until tops are cracked, 14-16 minutes. Remove to wire racks to cool.

2 COOKIES: 415 cal., 25g fat (6g sat. fat), 89mg chol., 332mg sod., 42g carb. (24g sugars, 2g fiber), 7g pro.

COFFEE CAKE MUFFIN MIX

Our local home-school group has an annual Christmas craft breakfast. Forty children signed up to come to my table and make this mix. It was so rewarding to see their excitement as they created a special gift to give.
—*Tamera Serafin, New Windsor, MD*

Prep: 15 min. • **Bake:** 20 min.
Makes: 1 dozen

- 1½ **cups all-purpose flour**
- ½ **cup sugar**
- 2 **tsp. baking powder**
- ½ **tsp. salt**
- ¼ **cup packed brown sugar**
- ¼ **cup chopped walnuts or pecans, toasted**
- 1 **tsp. ground cinnamon**

ADDITIONAL INGREDIENTS

- ½ **cup shortening**
- 1 **large egg, room temperature**
- ½ **cup 2% milk**
- 1 **Tbsp. butter, melted**

1. In a large bowl, whisk flour, sugar, baking powder and salt. Transfer to a 1-qt. resealable plastic bag. In a snack-size plastic bag, combine brown sugar, walnuts and cinnamon. Store bags in a cool, dry place or keep in the freezer up to 3 months.
2. To prepare muffins: Preheat oven to 350°. Place flour mixture in a large bowl. Cut in shortening until crumbly. In a small bowl, whisk egg and milk until blended. Add to the flour mixture; stir just until moistened. In a small bowl, mix brown sugar mixture with melted butter.
3. Fill greased or paper-lined muffin cups half full. Sprinkle with brown sugar mixture. Bake until a toothpick inserted in center comes out clean, 18-22 minutes. Cool 5 minutes before removing from pan to a wire rack. Serve warm.

1 MUFFIN: 216 cal., 11g fat (3g sat. fat), 19mg chol., 198mg sod., 26g carb. (13g sugars, 1g fiber), 3g pro.

Handmade

MUNCHABLE CRUNCHABLES

CASHEW BRITTLE

I like this quick and easy recipe because it doesn't require a candy thermometer. It also makes a wonderful gift.

—*Rhonda Glenn, Prince Frederick, MD*

Prep: 10 min.
Cook: 10 min. + chilling
Makes: ¾ lb.

- 2 tsp. butter, divided
- 1 cup sugar
- ½ cup light corn syrup
- 1 to 1½ cups salted cashew halves
- 1 tsp. baking soda
- 1 tsp. vanilla extract

1. Grease a baking sheet with 1 tsp. butter.
2. In a microwave-safe bowl, mix sugar and corn syrup; microwave, uncovered, on high for 3 minutes. Stir to dissolve sugar; microwave 2 minutes longer. Stir in the cashews and remaining butter; microwave on high for 40 seconds. Stir; continue microwaving in 20-second intervals until mixture turns a light amber color, about 1-2 minutes. (Mixture will be very hot.) Quickly stir in baking soda and vanilla until light and foamy.
3. Immediately pour onto prepared pan, spreading with a metal spatula; cool slightly. Refrigerate until brittle is set, 15-20 minutes.
4. Break candy into pieces. Store between layers of waxed paper in an airtight container.

1 OZ.: 187 cal., 7g fat (2g sat. fat), 1mg chol., 209mg sod., 30g carb. (24g sugars, 0 fiber), 2g pro.

CHEWY CARAMEL-COATED POPCORN

When I was a kid, my mom often made this recipe. I've adapted it to make a more chewy, gooey version. I get requests to make it for every event that I host. Packed into pretty decorative bags, it's always a welcome gift for friends and co-workers.

—*Shannon Dobos, Calgary, AB*

Takes: 25 min. • **Makes:** about 6 qt.

- 1½ cups butter, cubed
- 2⅔ cups packed light brown sugar
- 1 cup golden syrup
- 1 tsp. vanilla extract
- 24 cups popped popcorn

1. Line two 15x10x1-in. pans with parchment. In a large heavy saucepan, melt the butter over medium-high heat. Add brown sugar and syrup, stirring to dissolve brown sugar. Bring to a full rolling boil. Boil and stir 1 minute. Remove from heat and quickly stir in vanilla.
2. Pour caramel mixture over popcorn; stir lightly to coat. Using a rubber spatula, press the popcorn into prepared pans. Cool. Pull apart into pieces. Store in airtight containers.

NOTE: This recipe was tested with Lyles Golden Syrup.

1 CUP: 303 cal., 16g fat (8g sat. fat), 31mg chol., 216mg sod., 40g carb. (35g sugars, 1g fiber), 1g pro.

AUNT ROSE'S FANTASTIC BUTTER TOFFEE

I don't live in the country, but I love everything about it—especially good old-fashioned home cooking! Every year, you'll find me at our county fair, entering a different recipe contest. This toffee is a family favorite!

—*Kathy Dorman, Snover, MI*

Prep: 25 min.
Cook: 15 min.
Makes: about 2 lbs

- 2 cups unblanched whole almonds
- 11 oz. milk chocolate, chopped
- 1 cup butter, cubed
- 1 cup sugar
- 3 Tbsp. cold water

1. Preheat oven to 350°. In a shallow baking pan, toast the almonds until golden brown, 5-10 minutes, stirring occasionally. Cool. Pulse the chocolate in a food processor until finely ground (do not overprocess); transfer to a bowl. Pulse almonds in food processor until coarsely chopped. Sprinkle 1 cup almonds over bottom of a greased 15x10x1-in. pan. Sprinkle with 1 cup chocolate.

2. In a heavy saucepan, combine butter, sugar and water. Cook over medium heat until a candy thermometer reads 290° (soft-crack stage), stirring occasionally.

3. Immediately pour mixture over the almonds and chocolate in pan. Sprinkle with remaining chocolate and almonds. Refrigerate until set; break into pieces.

NOTE: We recommend that you test your candy thermometer before each use by bringing water to a boil; the thermometer should read 212°. Adjust your recipe temperature higher or lower based on your test.

1 OZ.: 177 cal., 13g fat (6g sat. fat), 17mg chol., 51mg sod., 14g carb. (12g sugars, 1g fiber), 3g pro.

HOMEMADE HELPER
Sometimes when you make toffee, the ingredients separate during cooking and there is a buttery layer on top and a thicker layer underneath. To save the batch of toffee, add about ½ cup hot water and stir until well blended. Continue cooking as directed.

KIDDIE CRUNCH MIX

This no-bake snack mix is a real treat for kids, and you can easily increase the amount to fit your needs. Place in individual plastic bags or pour some into colored ice cream cones and cover with plastic wrap for a fun presentation.
—*Kara de la Vega, Santa Rosa, CA*

. . . .

Takes: 10 min.
Makes: 6 cups

- 1 **cup plain or frosted animal crackers**
- 1 **cup bear-shaped crackers**
- 1 **cup miniature pretzels**
- 1 **cup salted peanuts**
- 1 **cup M&M's**
- 1 **cup yogurt- or chocolate-covered raisins**

In a bowl, combine all ingredients. Store in an airtight container.
½ **CUP:** 266 cal., 14g fat (5g sat. fat), 4mg chol., 159mg sod., 33g carb. (23g sugars, 3g fiber), 6g pro.

MAGIC WANDS

These fun and colorful magic wands don't take a magician to make. You can change the colors to fit any party theme.
—*Renee Schwebach, Dumont, MN*

. . . .

Prep: 25 min. + standing
Makes: 2 dozen

- 1½ **cups white baking chips**
- 1 **pkg. (10 oz.) pretzel rods**
  Colored candy stars or sprinkles
  Colored sugar or edible glitter

In a microwave, melt chips; stir until smooth. Dip each pretzel rod halfway into melted chips; allow excess to drip off. Sprinkle with candy stars and colored sugar. Place on waxed paper; let stand until dry. Store in an airtight container.
NOTE: Edible glitter is available from Wilton Industries. Visit wilton.com or call 800-794-5866.
1 **WAND:** 103 cal., 4g fat (2g sat. fat), 2mg chol., 164mg sod., 15g carb. (0 sugars, 0 fiber), 2g pro.

BANANAS FOSTER CRUNCH MIX

Bananas Foster is one of my favorite desserts. So I thought that a crunchy, snackable version would be a hit. It's heated in the microwave and takes just a few minutes to make.

—*David Dahlman, Chatsworth, CA*

Prep: 10 min.
Cook: 5 min. + cooling
Makes: 2½ qt.

    3   cups Honey Nut Chex
    3   cups Cinnamon Chex
    2¼ cups pecan halves
    1½ cups dried banana chips
    ⅓   cup butter, cubed
    ⅓   cup packed brown sugar
    ½   tsp. ground cinnamon
    ½   tsp. banana extract
    ½   tsp. rum extract

1. Place first four ingredients in a large microwave-safe bowl. Place butter, brown sugar and cinnamon in a small microwave-safe bowl; microwave on high for 2 minutes, stirring once. Stir in the extracts. Pour over the cereal mixture; toss to coat.

2. Microwave cereal mixture on high for 3 minutes, stirring every minute. Spread onto baking sheets to cool. Store in an airtight container.

¾ CUP: 358 cal., 24g fat (9g sat. fat), 14mg chol., 170mg sod., 36g carb. (18g sugars, 4g fiber), 4g pro.

CRANBERRY DARK CHOCOLATE TRAIL MIX

A close friend once gave me a jar of trail mix that was absolutely delicious. My re-creation comes pretty close to the original. This sweet and nutty mix is truly one of my favorite snacks!

—*Nancy Johnson, Laverne, OK*

Takes: 5 min.
Makes: 6 cups

    1   pkg. (10 oz.) dark chocolate chips
    1½ cups dried cranberries
        (about 8 oz.)
    1½ cups sliced almonds
    1   cup raisins
    1   cup coarsely chopped walnuts
    ½   cup pistachios

Toss together all ingredients. Store in airtight containers.

¼ CUP: 176 cal., 11g fat (3g sat. fat), 0 chol., 16mg sod., 21g carb. (15g sugars, 3g fiber), 3g pro.

CARAMEL CRISPY POPS

Ordinary crispy bars are fine for every day, but a bake sale calls for something special. I dress up mine with caramel and peanuts, then pop them on a stick to create a treat that's irresistible!

—*Linda Boufton, Dalton, OH*

Prep: 20 min. + cooling
Makes: 12 pops

    1   pkg. (14 oz.) caramels
    ¼   cup whole milk
    4   cups crisp rice cereal
    1   cup salted peanuts
    12 wooden pop sticks

1. Unwrap the caramels; place in a large heavy saucepan. Add milk; cook and stir over medium-low heat until melted. Remove from the heat. Stir in cereal and peanuts.

2. Press into a greased 8-in. square baking dish. Cool. Cut into 12 bars; gently insert a wooden pop stick into each bar. Store in an airtight container.

1 POP: 233 cal., 9g fat (2g sat. fat), 3mg chol., 219mg sod., 35g carb. (23g sugars, 1g fiber), 5g pro. DIABETIC EXCHANGES: 2 starch, 1½ fat.

CHOCOLATE, PEANUT & PRETZEL TOFFEE CRISPS

These crisps are the best combination of salty and sweet. They never last long because—trust me—they're addictive! Make the recipe the way it's written or sprinkle on any personal favorites.
—*Jennifer Butka, Livonia, MI*

. . . .

Prep: 25 min.
Bake: 10 min. + chilling
Makes: 2½ lbs.

- 40 Saltines
- ¾ cup butter, cubed
- ¾ cup packed brown sugar
- 1 tsp. vanilla extract
- 2 cups (12 oz.) semisweet chocolate chips
- 1 cup cocktail peanuts
- 1 cup broken pretzel sticks
- ¾ cup M&M's minis

1. Preheat oven to 350°. Line a 15x10x1-in. baking pan with foil; grease foil. Arrange Saltines in a single layer on foil.
2. In a large heavy saucepan, melt butter over medium heat. Stir in brown sugar. Bring to a boil; cook and stir until sugar is dissolved, 2-3 minutes. Remove from heat; stir in vanilla. Spread evenly over the crackers.
3. Bake until bubbly, 8-10 minutes. Immediately sprinkle with chocolate chips. Allow chips to soften 2 minutes, then spread over top. Sprinkle with peanuts, pretzels and M&M's minis; shake pan to settle toppings into the chocolate. Cool.
4. Refrigerate, uncovered, 1 hour or until set. Break into pieces. Store pieces in an airtight container.

1 OZ.: 146 cal., 9g fat (5g sat. fat), 11mg chol., 99mg sod., 16g carb. (12g sugars, 1g fiber), 2g pro.

SPICED ALMOND BRITTLE

I like sending homemade goodies to family and friends. When I couldn't decide between brittle and spiced nuts, I combined the two into one tasty bite.
—*Leslie Dixon, Boise, ID*

. . . .

Prep: 15 min.
Cook: 15 min. + cooling
Makes: 1¼ lbs.

- 1 cup sugar
- ¼ cup water
- ½ cup light corn syrup
- ¼ tsp. salt
- 1½ cups unblanched almonds
- 2 Tbsp. butter
- ½ tsp. pumpkin pie spice
- ¼ tsp. cayenne pepper
- ¼ tsp. dried rosemary, crushed
- ⅛ tsp. ground nutmeg
- 1 tsp. baking soda

1. Line a 15x10x1-in. pan with parchment. (Do not spray or grease.)
2. In a large heavy saucepan, combine the sugar, water, corn syrup and salt. Bring to a boil, stirring constantly to dissolve sugar. Using a pastry brush dipped in water, wash down the sides of the pan to eliminate sugar crystals. Cook, without stirring, over medium heat until a candy thermometer reads 260° (hard-ball stage).
3. Stir in almonds, butter and seasonings; cook until thermometer reads 300° (hard-crack stage), stirring frequently, about 8 minutes longer.
4. Remove from heat; stir in baking soda. (Mixture will foam.) Immediately pour onto prepared pan, spreading as thin as possible. Cool completely.
5. Break the brittle into pieces. Store candy between layers of waxed paper in airtight containers.

1 OZ.: 139 cal., 7g fat (1g sat. fat), 3mg chol., 109mg sod., 19g carb. (17g sugars, 1g fiber), 2g pro.

CRUNCHY GRANOLA PRETZEL STICKS

I love this healthier, portable snack that's sweet, crunchy and fun to make. If you don't have granola, use other cereals or nuts. You can even do bacon bits.
—*Kelly Silvers, Edmond, OK*

. . . .

Prep: 25 min. + standing
Makes: 2 dozen

- 1 **pkg. (12 oz.) dark chocolate chips**
- 24 **pretzel rods**
- 1 **cup granola without raisins**

1. In a microwave, melt chocolate chips in a 2-cup glass measuring cup; stir until smooth. Pour into one side of a large shallow dish.
2. Roll each pretzel halfway into chocolate. Allow excess coating to drip off, then sprinkle pretzels with granola. Place on waxed paper until set. Store in an airtight container.

1 PRETZEL STICK: 121 cal., 5g fat (3g sat. fat), 0 chol., 210mg sod., 19g carb. (8g sugars, 2g fiber), 3g pro.

SO-EASY SNACK MIX

I eat this tasty treat just as much as (if not more than) the kids! Have fun with it by adding other goodies into the mix, like nuts, cereal, pretzels and more.
—*Jeff King, Duluth, MN*

. . . .

Takes: 5 min.
Makes: 4 qt.

- 4 **cups miniature cheddar cheese fish-shaped crackers**
- 4 **cups golden raisins**
- 4 **cups dried cherries**
- 2 **cups yogurt-covered raisins**
- 2 **cups miniature pretzels**

Place all ingredients in a large bowl; toss to combine. Store in airtight containers.
½ CUP: 195 cal., 3g fat (1g sat. fat), 1mg chol., 104mg sod., 42g carb. (29g sugars, 2g fiber), 2g pro.

PHOTO GIFT TAGS

Create a personalized gift tag for everyone on your list. Use photos on the handmade tags instead of names. You'll easily remember to whom each gift belongs without having to handwrite "To" and "From" on the presents. Recipients will appreciate the heartfelt creative touch as much as the delicious treats you've tucked inside!

MATERIALS

Desired photos
Decorative card stock
Narrow satin ribbon
Two circle or square paper punches
   of slightly different sizes
Craft glue

DIRECTIONS

1. Using the smaller paper punch, punch out each desired photo. Using the larger paper punch, punch out a card stock shape for each photo.

2. If making circle tags, glue each photo to the center of a card stock circle. Glue the ends of a short length of ribbon to each tag to resemble the hanging loop of an ornament.

3. If making square tags, glue two short lengths of ribbon in a crisscross shape across the front of each card stock square. Glue each photo to the center of a card stock square. Tie a short length of ribbon into a bow and glue to the top of each tag to resemble the bow on a gift.

4. Let tags dry completely. Attach tags to gifts.

CHEDDAR-PECAN CRISPS

Lots of holiday treats are sweet. For a change of pace, I fill goodie bags with my cheese crackers. The recipe has a large yield, but you can freeze the dough logs to bake later.
—*Heather Necessary, Shamokin Dam, PA*

· ·

Prep: 25 min. + chilling
Bake: 15 min./batch
Makes: 24 dozen

  2 **cups unsalted butter, softened**
  4 **cups shredded sharp**
     cheddar cheese
4½ **cups all-purpose flour**
  1 **tsp. salt**
 ½ **tsp. garlic powder**
 ½ **tsp. cayenne pepper**
  1 **cup finely chopped**
     pecans, toasted

1. In a large bowl, cream the butter and cheese until light and fluffy. In another bowl, whisk flour, salt, garlic powder and cayenne; gradually beat into creamed mixture. Stir in pecans.

2. Shape into eight 10-in.-long logs. Wrap in plastic. Refrigerate 2 hours or until firm.

3. Preheat oven to 350°. Unwrap and cut dough crosswise into ¼-in. slices. Place 1 in. apart on ungreased baking sheets. Bake until edges are crisp and lightly browned, 12-14 minutes. Cool on pans 1 minute. Remove to wire racks to cool. Refrigerate in airtight containers.

FREEZE OPTION: Place wrapped logs in resealable plastic freezer bags; place in freezer. To use, unwrap frozen logs and cut into slices. If necessary, let dough stand 15 minutes at room temperature before cutting. Bake as directed, increasing time by 1-2 minutes.

NOTE: To toast nuts, bake in a shallow pan in a 350° oven for 5-10 minutes or cook in a skillet over low heat until lightly browned, stirring occasionally.

1 CRACKER: 27 cal., 2g fat (1g sat. fat), 5mg chol., 19mg sod., 2g carb. (0 sugars, 0 fiber), 1g pro.

Carrot Cake
Jam

Handmade
JAMS, JELLIES & MORE

CRAN-RASPBERRY JAM

This pretty ruby-colored jam makes fantastic gifts. Each fall, I pick up extra bags of cranberries to stash in the freezer so that I can make it year-round. My kids love it on peanut butter sandwiches.
—*Marjilee Booth, Chino Hills, CA*

Prep: 20 min.
Process: 10 min.
Makes: 6 half-pints

- 2 **pkg. (10 oz. each) frozen sweetened raspberries, thawed**
- 4 **cups fresh or frozen cranberries**
- 1 **pkg. (1¾ oz.) powdered fruit pectin**
- 5 **cups sugar**

1. Drain raspberries, reserving juice; add enough water to juice to measure 1½ cups. Pour into a Dutch oven. Add the raspberries and cranberries; stir in pectin. Bring to a full rolling boil over high heat, stirring constantly. Stir in sugar; return to a full rolling boil. Boil and stir 1 minute.
2. Remove from heat; skim off foam. Ladle hot mixture into six hot half-pint jars, leaving ¼-in. headspace. Remove air bubbles and adjust headspace, if necessary, by adding hot mixture. Wipe rims. Center lids on jars; screw on bands until fingertip tight.
3. Place jars into canner with simmering water, ensuring that they are completely covered with water. Bring to a boil; process for 10 minutes. Remove the jars and cool.
NOTE: The processing time listed is for altitudes of 1,000 feet or less. Add 1 minute to the processing time for each 1,000 feet of additional altitude.
2 TBSP.: 96 cal., 0 fat (0 sat. fat), 0 chol., 0 sod., 25g carb. (23g sugars, 1g fiber), 0 pro.

CARROT CAKE JAM

For a change of pace from berry jams, try this unique option. Spread on a bagel with cream cheese, it tastes almost as good as real carrot cake!
—*Rachelle Stratton, Rock Springs, WY*

Prep: 45 min.
Process: 5 min.
Makes: 8 half-pints

- 1 **can (20 oz.) unsweetened crushed pineapple, undrained**
- 1½ **cups shredded carrots**
- 1½ **cups chopped peeled ripe pears**
- 3 **Tbsp. lemon juice**
- 1 **tsp. ground cinnamon**
- ¼ **tsp. ground cloves**
- ¼ **tsp. ground nutmeg**
- 1 **pkg. (1¾ oz.) powdered fruit pectin**
- 6½ **cups sugar**

1. Place first seven ingredients in a large saucepan; bring to a boil. Reduce heat; simmer, covered, until pears are tender, 15-20 minutes, stirring occasionally. Stir in pectin. Bring to a full rolling boil over high heat, stirring constantly. Stir in sugar; return to a full rolling boil. Boil and stir 1 minute.
2. Remove from heat; skim off foam. Ladle hot mixture into eight hot sterilized half-pint jars, leaving ¼-in. headspace. Remove the air bubbles and adjust headspace, if necessary, by adding hot mixture. Wipe rims. Center lids on jars; screw on bands until fingertip tight.
3. Place jars into canner with simmering water, ensuring that they are completely covered with water. Bring to a boil; process for 5 minutes. Remove the jars and cool.
NOTE: The processing time listed is for altitudes of 1,000 feet or less. Add 1 minute to the processing time for each 1,000 feet of additional altitude.
2 TBSP.: 88 cal., 0 fat (0 sat. fat), 0 chol., 2mg sod., 23g carb. (22g sugars, 0 fiber), 0 pro.

SWEET & SPICY PICKLED RED SEEDLESS GRAPES

Most people don't think about grapes when planning a homemade gift, so these flavor-packed fruits are a real surprise. They're perfect on an antipasto platter or cheese tray.

—Cheryl Perry, Hertford, NC

Prep: 35 min.
Process: 10 min.
Makes: 4 pints

- 5 cups seedless red grapes
- 4 jalapeno peppers, seeded and sliced
- 2 Tbsp. minced fresh gingerroot
- 2 cinnamon sticks (3 in.), halved
- 4 whole star anise
- 2 tsp. coriander seeds
- 2 tsp. mustard seed
- 2 cups packed brown sugar
- 2 cups white wine vinegar
- 1 cup water
- 1 cup dry red wine
- 1½ tsp. canning salt

1. Pack grapes into four hot 1-pint jars to within 1½ in. of the top. Divide jalapenos, ginger, cinnamon, star anise, coriander seeds and mustard seed among jars.
2. In a large saucepan, combine brown sugar, vinegar, water, wine and canning salt. Bring to a boil; cook until liquid is reduced to 3 cups, 15-18 minutes.
3. Carefully ladle hot liquid over grape mixture, leaving ½-in. headspace. Remove the air bubbles and adjust headspace, if necessary, by adding hot liquid. Wipe rims. Center lids on jars; screw on bands until fingertip tight.
4. Place jars into canner, ensuring that they are completely covered with water. Bring to a boil; process for 10 minutes. Remove jars and cool.

NOTE: The processing time listed is for altitudes of 1,000 feet or less. For altitudes up to 3,000 feet, add 5 minutes; 6,000 feet, add 10 minutes; 8,000 feet, add 15 minutes; 10,000 feet, add 20 minutes.

¼ CUP: 32 cal., 0 fat (0 sat. fat), 0 chol., 7mg sod., 0 carb. (7g sugars, 0 fiber), 0 pro.

GENTLEMAN'S WHISKEY BACON JAM

You can slather this smoky jam on pretty much anything. It lasts only a week in the fridge, so I freeze small amounts for quick gifts and late-night snacks.
—*Colleen Delawder, Herndon, VA*

Prep: 15 min.
Cook: 30 min.
Makes: 3 cups

1½	lbs. thick-sliced bacon strips, finely chopped
8	shallots, finely chopped
1	large sweet onion, finely chopped
2	garlic cloves, minced
1	tsp. chili powder
½	tsp. paprika
¼	tsp. kosher salt
¼	tsp. pepper
½	cup whiskey
½	cup maple syrup
¼	cup balsamic vinegar
½	cup packed brown sugar
	Assorted crackers

1. In a large skillet, cook the bacon over medium heat until crisp. Drain on paper towels. Discard all but 2 Tbsp. drippings. Add shallots and onion to the drippings; cook over medium heat until caramelized, stirring occasionally.
2. Stir in garlic; cook 30 seconds. Add the seasonings. Remove from heat; stir in whiskey and maple syrup. Increase heat to high; bring to a boil and cook 3 minutes, stirring constantly. Add the vinegar and brown sugar; cook another 3 minutes, continuing to stir constantly.
3. Add crumbled bacon; reduce heat to low, and cook 12 minutes, stirring every few minutes. Allow jam to cool slightly. Pulse half of the jam in a food processor until smooth; stir puree into remaining jam. Serve with assorted crackers.

2 TBSP.: 112 cal., 8g fat (3g sat. fat), 10mg chol., 118mg sod., 7g carb. (5g sugars, 0 fiber), 2g pro.

CHUNKY FRUIT & NUT RELISH

I tuck a jar of this colorful condiment alongside the fudge and cookies in my gift baskets. Packed with chopped pecans, the fruit relish is delicious served with ham or poultry.

—Donna Brockett, Kingfisher, OK

Prep: 5 min.
Cook: 10 min. + chilling
Makes: 6 cups

- 2 pkg. (12 oz. each) fresh or frozen cranberries
- 1½ cups sugar
- 1 cup orange juice
- 1 can (15¼ oz.) sliced peaches, drained and cut up
- 1 cup chopped pecans
- ¾ cup pineapple tidbits
- ½ cup golden raisins

1. In a large saucepan, bring cranberries, sugar and orange juice to a boil, stirring occasionally. Reduce heat; simmer, uncovered, until the cranberries pop, 8-10 minutes.

2. Remove from heat; stir in peaches, pecans, pineapple and raisins. Cool. Cover and refrigerate at least 3 hours.

¼ CUP: 114 cal., 4g fat (0 sat. fat), 0 chol., 3mg sod., 21g carb. (19g sugars, 1g fiber), 1g pro.

CRANBERRY HONEY BUTTER

Need a unique hostess gift? Spending the weekend at a friend's home? Bring them something better than a bottle of wine or a candle—this easy-to-whip-up treat!

—Arisa Cupp, Warren, OR

Takes: 10 min.
Makes: 24 servings

- 1 cup butter, softened
- ⅓ cup finely chopped dried cranberries
- ¼ cup honey
- 2 tsp. grated orange zest
- ⅛ tsp. kosher salt

In a small bowl, beat all ingredients until blended. Store in an airtight container in the refrigerator up to 2 weeks or freeze up to 3 months.

1 TBSP.: 75 cal., 8g fat (5g sat. fat), 20mg chol., 71mg sod., 2g carb. (2g sugars, 0 fiber), 0 pro.

> **HOMEMADE HELPER**
> Try replacing the dried cranberries and orange zest with dried cherries and lime zest, or dried blueberries and lemon zest. If you replace the honey with maple syrup, this pairs perfectly with a stack of fluffy pancakes.

HOMEMADE PEAR HONEY

Pear honey is an old recipe that's been passed down through families. We especially like it with hot biscuits and butter. It's also good on pound cake or even ice cream. Make sure the pears you use are very firm.

—*Charlotte McDaniel, Jacksonville, AL*

Prep: 15 min.
Cook: 45 min.
Makes: 6 half-pints

- 8 medium pears, peeled and quartered
- 4 cups sugar
- 1 can (20 oz.) crushed pineapple, drained

1. Place pears in a food processor; process until finely chopped. In a Dutch oven, combine pears and sugar; bring to a boil. Reduce heat; simmer, uncovered, 45 minutes, stirring occasionally. Stir in pineapple; cook and stir 5 minutes longer.
2. Remove from heat. Ladle hot liquid into hot half-pint jars; wipe rims. Seal and allow to cool. Refrigerate up to 2 weeks.
2 TBSP.: 91 cal., 0 fat (0 sat. fat), 0 chol., 1mg sod., 24g carb. (22g sugars, 1g fiber), 0 pro.

EASY STRAWBERRY BUTTER

After picking strawberries for the first time, I developed this fruity, spreadable butter. Try other fruit spreads using raspberries, blackberries or even seedless jams like apricot.

—*Julie Herrera-Lemler, Rochester, MN*

Takes: 5 min.
Makes: 2¼ cups

- 6 large fresh strawberries, stems removed and room temperature
- 1 cup butter, softened
- ¾ to 1 cup confectioners' sugar

Pulse strawberries in a food processor until chopped. Add butter and ½ cup confectioners' sugar; process until blended. Add enough remaining confectioners' sugar to reach a spreading consistency and the desired level of sweetness. Store in the refrigerator for up to 1 week.
1 TBSP.: 56 cal., 5g fat (3g sat. fat), 14mg chol., 41mg sod., 3g carb. (3g sugars, 0 fiber), 0 pro.

CHRISTMAS PICKLES

My pickle recipe was adapted from one a dear family friend shared. These morsels are delicious any time of year, but the green, red and white hues of the pickles, cherries and onions make them ideal for holiday gift-giving.

—*Patricia Martin, Shelbyville, TN*

Prep: 10 min.
Cook: 25 min. + chilling
Makes: 6½ qt.

- 1 gallon whole dill pickles
- 11¼ cups sugar
- 1 cup white vinegar
- 1 Tbsp. mustard seed
- 1 Tbsp. whole cloves
- 3 to 4 jalapeno peppers, chopped
- 4 to 5 garlic cloves, minced
- 4 to 5 whole cinnamon sticks
- 1 lb. whole candied cherries
- 3 jars (15 oz. each) pearl onions, drained
- 1 tsp. olive oil

1. Drain pickles, reserving juice; set juice aside. Cut pickles into ½-in. slices; set aside. In a large stockpot, combine sugar, vinegar, mustard seed, cloves, peppers, garlic, cinnamon sticks and pickle juice.
2. Cook over medium heat until the sugar is dissolved, about 10 minutes, stirring occasionally. Bring to a boil. Reduce heat; simmer, uncovered, 10 minutes. Remove from heat; cool slightly. Discard the cinnamon sticks.
3. In a large bowl, combine the cherries, onions and pickle slices. Pour liquid over pickle mixture. Stir in oil.
4. Cover and refrigerate for 48 hours, stirring occasionally. Divide mixture among jars. Cover and store in the refrigerator up to 1 month.
NOTE: Wear disposable gloves when cutting hot peppers; the oils can burn skin. Avoid touching your face.
¼ CUP: 99 cal., 0 fat (0 sat. fat), 0 chol., 55mg sod., 25g carb. (23g sugars, 0 fiber), 0 pro.

HOME MADE

BBQ SPICED KETCHUP

I once bought my ketchup-loving husband a bottle of flavored ketchup from a fancy store. He loved the gift, but I didn't love the price. So I experimented and came up with my very own spiced ketchup. Now my husband and I are both happy! I actually kept two half-pint jars in my refrigerator without processing because I knew we would go through them fast—and we did!

—*Nancy Murphy, Mount Dora, FL*

Prep: 35 min.
Process: 20 min.
Makes: 5 half-pints

- 4 cups ketchup
- 1 cup cider vinegar
- ¼ cup packed dark brown sugar
- ¼ cup molasses
- 2 Tbsp. honey
- 1 Tbsp. Worcestershire sauce
- 2 tsp. kosher salt
- 2 tsp. ground mustard
- ½ tsp. pepper
- ½ tsp. celery seed
- ½ tsp. garlic powder
- ½ tsp. paprika
- ½ tsp. chili powder

1. In a Dutch oven, combine all of the ingredients. Slowly bring to a boil over medium-high heat. Reduce heat; simmer, uncovered, until mixture is thickened, 25-30 minutes.
2. Carefully ladle hot mixture into five hot ½-pint jars, leaving ½-in. headspace. Remove the air bubbles and adjust headspace, if necessary, by adding hot mixture. Wipe rims. Center lids on jars; screw on bands until fingertip tight.
3. Place jars into canner with simmering water, ensuring that they are completely covered with water. Bring to a boil; process for 20 minutes. Remove the jars and cool.
NOTE: The processing time listed is for altitudes of 1,000 feet or less. For altitudes up to 3,000 feet, add 5 minutes; 6,000 feet, add 10 minutes; 8,000 feet, add 15 minutes; 10,000 feet, add 20 minutes.
2 TBSP.: 37 cal., 0 fat (0 sat. fat), 0 chol., 370mg sod., 9g carb. (9g sugars, 0 fiber), 0 pro.

TANGY PICKLED MUSHROOMS

Home-canned pickled mushrooms are a great addition to any pantry. They're ideal for cocktails, appetizers, salads and relish trays. What a surprise gift!

—*Jill Hihn, West Grove, PA*

Prep: 50 min.
Process: 20 min./batch
Makes: 8 pints

- 5 lbs. small fresh mushrooms
- 2 large onions, halved and sliced
- 2 cups white vinegar
- 1½ cups canola oil
- ¼ cup sugar
- 2 Tbsp. canning salt
- 3 garlic cloves, minced
- 1½ tsp. pepper
- ¼ tsp. dried tarragon

1. Place all ingredients in a stockpot. Bring to a boil. Reduce heat; simmer, uncovered, 10 minutes. Carefully ladle hot mixture into eight hot 1-pint jars, leaving ½-in. headspace.
2. Remove air bubbles and adjust headspace, if necessary, by adding hot mixture. Wipe rims. Center lids on jars; screw on bands until fingertip tight. Place jars into canner, ensuring that they are completely covered with water. Bring to a boil. Process for 20 minutes. Remove jars and cool.
NOTE: The processing time listed is for altitudes of 1,000 feet or less. For altitudes up to 3,000 feet, add 5 minutes; 6,000 feet, add 10 minutes; 8,000 feet, add 15 minutes; 10,000 feet, add 20 minutes.
¼ CUP: 18 cal., 1g fat (0 sat. fat), 0 chol., 35mg sod., 2g carb. (1g sugars, 1g fiber), 1g pro.

A GIFT OF SPRING CANNING JARS

You put up jams, jellies, pickles and preserves with a lot of love. So why not dress up the jars containing the fruits of your labor? These labels and jar toppers are a snap to make and will make the most of your handmade gift.

Canning jars and lids
Card stock
Fabric scraps
Buttons
Striped twine
Scalloped-edge circle punch
    (1 in. or desired size)
Hole punch
Pinking shears

1. Use a circle punch to cut round labels from card stock. Mark and decorate labels as desired.
2. Use a hole punch to punch a hole at the top of each label.
3. With pinking shears, cut a scalloped circle of fabric about 3 in. wider in diameter than the canning jar lid.
4. Cover the lid with fabric and twist the band in place over it. Trim fabric if needed.
5. Thread twine through one hole of a button and the hole in a label. Wrap twine around the lid band and up through the opposite hole of the button. Tie in place.

HOMEMADE LEMON CURD

Lemon curd is a scrumptious spread for scones, biscuits or other baked goods. You can find it in larger grocery stores alongside the jams and jellies or with the baking supplies, but we like making it from scratch.
—*Mark Hagen, Milwaukee, WI*

Prep: 20 min. + chilling
Makes: 1⅔ cups

3   large eggs
1   cup sugar
½   cup lemon juice (about 2 lemons)
¼   cup butter, cubed
1   Tbsp. grated lemon zest

In a small heavy saucepan over medium heat, whisk eggs, sugar and lemon juice until blended. Add butter and lemon zest; cook, whisking constantly, until mixture is thickened and coats the back of a metal spoon. Transfer to a small bowl; cool 10 minutes. Refrigerate, covered, until cold.
2 TBSP.: 110 cal., 5g fat (3g sat. fat), 52mg chol., 45mg sod., 16g carb. (16g sugars, 0 fiber), 2g pro.

> ### READER RAVE
> *"I love lemon curd! In the supermarkets near me, however, it is expensive, so thank you for this recipe. I will make it today, and tomorrow use it in a great dessert."*
> —AHTINAHW, TASTEOFHOME.COM

Handmade
SPICES &
SEASONINGS

MOMMA WATTS' CRAZY HERBY SALT BLEND

This recipe for a delicious salt blend came from my best friend Annabelle's mom, Mary Watts—Momma Watts to me and my friends! Last year I made it to give as gifts, and it was wonderfully received.
—*Ava Romero, South San Francisco, CA*

Takes: 10 min.
Makes: about 2 cups

- 2 Tbsp. dried rosemary, crushed
- 1 to 2 Tbsp. fennel seed
- 2 cups kosher salt
- ½ tsp. garlic powder

In a spice grinder or with a mortar and pestle, grind rosemary and fennel until powdery. Stir rosemary mixture into salt; add garlic powder. Transfer seasoning mix to clean 3- or 4-oz. jars. Store in a cool dry place up to 6 months.
¼ TSP.: 0 cal., 0 fat (0 sat. fat), 0 chol., 480mg sod., 0 carb. (0 sugars, 0 fiber), 0 pro.

ALL-PURPOSE MEAT SEASONING

My terrific mother-in-law gave me this meat seasoning recipe. I sprinkle it over boneless pork tenderloin before baking.
—*Rebekah Widrick, Beaver Falls, NY*

Takes: 10 min.
Makes: 1½ cups

- ¾ cup packed brown sugar
- 3 Tbsp. kosher salt
- 3 Tbsp. paprika
- 3 Tbsp. chili powder
- 2 Tbsp. garlic powder
- 2 Tbsp. onion powder
- 1 Tbsp. ground cumin
- 1 Tbsp. dried oregano

Combine all ingredients. Transfer to an airtight container. Store in a cool dry place up to 1 year.
NOTE: The seasoning caramelizes quickly when the meat is seared in a skillet.
1 TSP.: 15 cal., 0 fat (0 sat. fat), 0 chol., 301mg sod., 4g carb. (3g sugars, 0 fiber), 0 pro.

STRAWBERRY-BASIL VINEGAR

The mild, fruity flavor of this vinegar complements any tossed salad.
—*Taste of Home Test Kitchen*

Prep: 30 min. + standing
Process: 10 min.
Makes: 5 half-pints

- 4 cups fresh strawberries, hulled
- 4 cups white wine vinegar
- 1 Tbsp. grated lemon zest
- 1 cup loosely packed basil leaves

1. Place strawberries in a food processor; cover and process until pureed. Transfer to a glass bowl; add vinegar and lemon zest. Place ¼ cup basil in a small bowl.
2. With a mortar or a wooden spoon, crush basil until aromas are released. Repeat with remaining basil; stir into strawberry mixture. Cover and let stand in a cool, dark place for up to 3 days, stirring once daily.
3. Line a strainer with four layers of cheesecloth or one coffee filter and place over a large saucepan. Strain the vinegar into pan (do not press out the solids). Discard solids.
4. Heat vinegar to 180° over medium heat. Carefully ladle hot mixture into hot half-pint jars, leaving ¼-in. headspace. Wipe rims. Center lids on jars; screw on bands until fingertip tight.
5. Place jars into canner with simmering water, ensuring that they are completely covered with water. Bring to a boil; process for 10 minutes. Remove jars and cool.
NOTE: The processing time listed is for altitudes of 1,000 feet or less. Add 1 minute to the processing time for each 1,000 feet of additional altitude.
1 TBSP.: 6 cal., 0 fat (0 sat. fat), 0 chol., 0 sod., 1g carb. (0 sugars, 0 fiber), 0 pro.

CHILI-SCENTED SEASONING

This pleasantly mild seasoning blend is a great way to perk up fish, poultry and meat. Set it on the table, just as you would salt.

—*Millie Osburn, Winona, MO*

Takes: 5 min
Makes: 1 cup

6	Tbsp. onion powder
3	Tbsp. poultry seasoning
3	Tbsp. paprika
2	Tbsp. ground mustard
1	Tbsp. garlic powder
2	tsp. dried oregano, crushed
1	tsp. chili powder
1	tsp. black pepper
¼	tsp. cayenne pepper

Combine all ingredients. Store in an airtight container.
½ **TSP.:** 4 cal., 0 fat (0 sat. fat), 0 chol., 1mg sod., 1g carb. (0 sugars, 0 fiber), 0 pro.

VANILLA SUGAR

Sprinkle vanilla sugar on just about anything to make things a bit more special. I stir mine into angel food cake batter, cookie dough, rice pudding and even fruit sauces.

—*Jackie Termont, Ruther Glen, VA*

Prep: 5 min. + standing
Makes: 2 cups

2	cups sugar
1	vanilla bean

Place sugar in an airtight container. Split vanilla bean lengthwise. Using the tip of a sharp knife, scrape seeds from the center into sugar; add bean. Seal container and shake until blended. Let stand, covered, at least 1 week. Use as regular granulated sugar, discarding the vanilla bean as it loses its flavor.
1 **TSP.:** 16 cal., 0 fat (0 sat. fat), 0 chol., 0 sod., 4g carb. (4g sugars, 0 fiber), 0 pro.

SAVORY POPCORN SEASONING

I love tossing this combination of herbs and seasonings with popcorn. Cayenne pepper adds a bit of heat to the late-night treat. It's a fun hostess gift.

—*Janice Campbell, Elmendorf AFB, AK*

Takes: 10 min.
Makes: 24 batches (about ¼ cup)

1	Tbsp. garlic powder
1	Tbsp. dried parsley flakes
1½	tsp. dried basil
1½	tsp. dried marjoram
1½	tsp. dried thyme
1½	tsp. pepper
¾	tsp. cayenne pepper

ADDITIONAL INGREDIENTS FOR POPCORN

2	cups air-popped popcorn
1½	tsp. butter, melted

1. Combine first seven ingredients. Store in an airtight container up to 6 months.
2. To prepare popcorn: Combine the popcorn, butter and ½ tsp. seasoning; toss to coat.
2 **CUPS SEASONED POPCORN.:** 114 cal., 6g fat (4g sat. fat), 15mg chol., 59mg sod., 13g carb. (0 sugars, 3g fiber), 2g pro.

SHOWN ON PAGE 54
GINGERBREAD-SPICED SYRUP

Here's a wonderful treat! Simply stir a tablespoon into coffee, tea or cider, drizzle it over pancakes, hot cereal or yogurt. You can also use it as a glaze for chicken or pork chops.

—*Darlene Brenden, Salem, OR*

Prep: 20 min.
Cook: 30 min. + cooling
Makes: 2 cups

- 2 cinnamon sticks (3 in.), broken into pieces
- 16 whole cloves
- 3 Tbsp. coarsely chopped fresh gingerroot
- 1 tsp. whole allspice
- 1 tsp. whole peppercorns
- 2 cups sugar
- 2 cups water
- 2 Tbsp. honey
- 1 tsp. ground nutmeg

1. Place the first five ingredients on a double thickness of cheesecloth; bring up corners of cloth and tie with string to form a bag.
2. In a large saucepan, combine sugar, water, honey, nutmeg and spice bag; bring to a boil. Reduce heat; simmer, uncovered, until syrup reaches desired consistency, 30-45 minutes.
3. Remove from the heat; cool to room temperature. Discard spice bag; transfer syrup to airtight containers. Store in the refrigerator for up to 1 month.
2 TBSP.: 108 cal., 0 fat (0 sat. fat), 0 chol., 0 sod., 28g carb. (27g sugars, 0 fiber), 0 pro.

CRANBERRY ORANGE VINEGAR

I enjoy making an assortment of vinegars, but this Christmasy one is a favorite. The longer the cranberries and oranges sit in the vinegar, the more intensely flavored the mixture becomes.

—*Kathy Rairigh, Milford, IN*

Prep: 10 min. + standing
Makes: 6 cups

- 6 cups white wine vinegar
- 1 pkg. (12 oz.) fresh or frozen cranberries, chopped
- 3 medium oranges, sectioned and chopped

1. In a large saucepan, heat vinegar to just below the boiling point. In a large bowl, lightly mash the cranberries and oranges; add heated vinegar. Cover and let stand in a cool, dark place for 10 days.
2. Strain mixture through a cheesecloth and discard pulp. Pour into sterilized jars or decorative bottles. Seal tightly. Store in a cool, dark place.
1 TBSP.: 9 cal., 0 fat (0 sat. fat), 0 chol., 0 sod., 2g carb. (0 sugars, 0 fiber), 0 pro.

CRANBERRY ORANGE VINAIGRETTE

When I give bottles of my Cranberry Orange Vinegar, I'm certain to include this recipe.

—*Kathy Rairigh, Milford, IN*

Takes: 10 min.
Makes: 1¼ cups

- ½ cup Cranberry Orange Vinegar (recipe at left) or raspberry vinegar
- ¼ cup maple syrup
- ½ tsp. salt
- ½ tsp. grated orange zest
- ½ tsp. ground mustard
- ⅛ tsp. coarsely ground pepper
- ½ cup canola oil
- ½ tsp. poppy seeds

In a blender, combine the first six ingredients. Cover and process for 1 minute. While processing, gradually add oil in a steady stream. Stir in poppy seeds. Store in the refrigerator.
2 TBSP.: 120 cal., 11g fat (1g sat. fat), 0 chol., 119mg sod., 5g carb. (4g sugars, 0 fiber), 0 pro.

ZIPPY DRY RUB

Bottles of this spicy blend are fun to share with family and friends. It's a mixture with broad appeal since the rub can be used on all meats or added to rice while it is cooking for a boost of flavor.

—*Gaynelle Fritsch, Welches, OR*

Takes: 5 min.
Makes: about 2½ Tbsp.

- 1 **Tbsp. salt**
- 1 **tsp. mustard seed**
- 1 **tsp. pepper**
- 1 **tsp. chili powder**
- 1 **tsp. paprika**
- ½ **tsp. ground cumin**
- ½ **tsp. dried coriander**
- ¼ **tsp. garlic powder**

Combine all ingredients; store in an airtight container. Rub desired amount onto surface of uncooked meat. Cover meat and refrigerate at least 4 hours before grilling.

¼ TSP.: 2 cal., 0 fat (0 sat. fat), 0 chol., 237mg sod., 0 carb. (0 sugars, 0 fiber), 0 pro.

MAKE A GIFT MIX COMBO

Considering a creative new way to package spices, seasonings and mixes? Look for transparent ornaments at your local craft store. Spoon your mixes into two or three ornaments for memorable gift set.

SALT-FREE HERB BLEND

I rely on a handful of seasonings, from paprika to poppy seeds, to make this salt-free mix. It's wonderful on vegetables such as corn on the cob, and it perks up poultry, beef and pork, too.
—*Eva Bailey, Olive Hill, KY*

Takes: 5 min.
Makes: ⅓ cup

- 4 tsp. sesame seeds
- 2 tsp. celery seed
- 2 tsp. dried marjoram
- 2 tsp. poppy seeds
- 2 tsp. coarsely ground pepper
- 1½ tsp. dried parsley flakes
- 1 tsp. onion powder
- 1 tsp. dried thyme
- ½ tsp. garlic powder
- ½ tsp. paprika

Combine all ingredients. Store in an airtight container up to 6 months.
¼ TSP.: 3 cal., 0 fat (0 sat. fat), 0 chol., 0 sod., 0 carb. (0 sugars, 0 fiber), 0 pro.

SAVORY STEAK RUB

Marjoram stars in this recipe. I use the rub on a variety of beef cuts because it locks in the natural juices of the meat for truly mouthwatering results.
—*Donna Brockett, Kingfisher, OK*

Takes: 5 min.
Makes: ¼ cup

- 1 Tbsp. dried majoram
- 1 Tbsp. dried basil
- 2 tsp. garlic powder
- 2 tsp. dried thyme
- 1 tsp. dried rosemary, crushed
- ¾ tsp. dried oregano

Combine all ingredients; store in an airtight container. Rub over steaks before grilling or broiling. Mixture will season four to five steaks.
1 TBSP.: 12 cal., 0 fat (0 sat. fat), 0 chol., 2mg sod., 3g carb. (0 sugars, 1g fiber), 1g pro.

HOMEMADE CAJUN SEASONING

We in Louisiana love seasoned foods. I use this in gravy, over meats and with salads. It makes an excellent gift for teachers. Many have asked for the recipe.
—*Onietta Loewer, Branch, LA*

Takes: 5 min.
Makes: about 3½ cups

- 1 carton (26 oz.) salt
- 2 containers (1 oz. each) cayenne pepper
- ⅓ cup pepper
- ⅓ cup chili powder
- 3 Tbsp. garlic powder

Combine all ingredients; store in airtight containers. Use to season pork, chicken, seafood, steaks or vegetables.
¼ TSP.: 1 cal., 0 fat (0 sat. fat), 0 chol., 433mg sod., 0 carb. (0 sugars, 0 fiber), 0 pro.

LEMON-GINGER SALT

Sprinkle a little bit of this zingy lemon-ginger combo on hot veggies for a change-of-pace twist.
—Taste of Home *Test Kitchen*

Prep: 10 min.
Bake: 20 min. + cooling
Makes: 1 cup

- ¾ cup kosher salt
- ½ cup grated lemon zest (from about 5 large lemons)
- 1 tsp. ground ginger
- 2 Tbsp. lemon juice

Preheat oven to 200°. Pulse salt, lemon zest and ginger in a food processor until blended. Transfer to an 8-in. square baking dish. Stir in the lemon juice. Bake, stirring occasionally, until dry, 20-25 minutes. Cool completely. Stir with a fork to break up. Store in an airtight container in a cool, dry place for up to 3 months.
¼ TSP.: 0 cal., 0 fat (0 sat. fat), 0 chol., 360mg sod., 0 carb. (0 sugars, 0 fiber), 0 pro.

• • •

Handmade
BAKED
DELIGHTS

CINNAMON ROLLS

My wife tells people that after I retired, I went from being the breadwinner to the bread baker! It all started with a simple college class. Now my breads and rolls are favorites of friends and family.
—*Ben Middleton, Walla Walla, WA*

Prep: 20 min. + rising
Bake: 25 min.
Makes: 2 dozen

- 2 pkg. (¼ oz. each) active dry yeast
- ½ cup sugar, divided
- 1 cup warm water (110° to 115°)
- 1 cup whole milk
- 6 Tbsp. butter
- 7 to 7½ cups all-purpose flour
- 3 large eggs, room temperature, beaten
- 1 tsp. salt

FILLING
- ¼ cup butter, softened
- 5 tsp. ground cinnamon
- ¾ cup packed brown sugar
- ¾ cup raisins or dried currants
  Vanilla frosting, optional

1. In a large bowl, dissolve the yeast and 1 Tbsp. sugar in water. In a saucepan, heat milk and butter to 110°-115°; add to yeast mixture. Stir in 3 cups flour, eggs, salt and remaining sugar. Stir in enough remaining flour to make a soft dough.
2. Turn out onto a lightly floured surface. Knead dough until smooth and elastic, 6-8 minutes. Place in a greased bowl, turning once to grease top. Cover and let rise in a warm place until doubled, about 1 hour.
3. Punch dough down and divide in half. Roll each half into a 15x12-in. rectangle. Brush with softened butter. Combine the cinnamon, sugar and raisins or currants; sprinkle evenly over rectangle. Roll up tightly, jelly-roll style, starting with the long side. Slice each roll into 12 pieces. Place in two greased standard muffin pans. Cover and let rise until doubled, about 30 minutes.
4. Bake at 350° until rolls are golden brown, 25-30 minutes. Cool in pans for 5 minutes; invert onto a wire rack. Top with frosting if desired. Serve warm.
1 CINNAMON ROLL: 248 cal., 6g fat (3g sat. fat), 41mg chol., 164mg sod., 43g carb. (15g sugars, 1g fiber), 5g pro.

CHOCOLATE CHIP MINI MUFFINS

I bake a lot of different muffins, but this is the recipe I use the most. Their small size makes them difficult to resist!
—*Joanne Shew Chuk, St. Benedict, SK*

Prep: 15 min.
Bake: 10 min.
Makes: about 3 dozen

- ½ cup sugar
- ¼ cup shortening
- 1 large egg, room temperature
- ½ cup 2% milk
- ½ tsp. vanilla extract
- 1 cup all-purpose flour
- ½ tsp. baking soda
- ½ tsp. baking powder
- ¼ tsp. salt
- ⅔ cup miniature semisweet chocolate chips

1. In a large bowl, cream sugar and shortening until light and fluffy. Beat in egg, then milk and vanilla. Combine the flour, baking soda, baking powder and salt; add to creamed mixture just until combined. Fold in chocolate chips.
2. Spoon about 1 Tbsp. of batter into each greased or paper-lined mini-muffin cup. Bake at 375° until a toothpick inserted in the center comes out clean, 10-13 minutes. Cool in pans 5 minutes before removing to wire racks.
2 MINI MUFFINS: 110 cal., 5g fat (2g sat. fat), 13mg chol., 87mg sod., 15g carb. (9g sugars, 1g fiber), 2g pro.

> **READER RAVE**
> *"These little muffins are so delicious!! They're easy to make. I always have all the ingredients on hand. Plus everyone can't wait till they come out of the oven!*
> —EFWYNNE, TASTEOFHOME.COM

CHERRY ALMOND MINI LOAVES

Plenty of good things come in these tiny loaves that feature golden raisins and cherries. There's a sweet surprise—the creamy almond filling—in every bite.
—*Connie Simon, Reed City, MO*

Prep: 45 min. + rising
Bake: 20 min.
Makes: 12 mini loaves

- ¾ cup whole milk
- ¾ cup butter, divided
- ½ cup sugar
- 1 tsp. salt
- 2 pkg. (¼ oz. each) active dry yeast
- ¼ cup warm water (110° to 115°)
- 2 large eggs, room temperature
- 1 large egg yolk, room temperature
- 5½ to 6 cups all-purpose flour
- 1½ cups golden raisins
- 1⅓ cups candied cherry halves
- 1 tsp. grated orange zest

FILLING
- 1 pkg. (8 oz.) almond paste
- ½ cup sugar
- 1 large egg white
  Confectioners' sugar

1. In a large saucepan, combine milk, ½ cup butter, sugar and salt. Cook over low heat until butter is melted; stir until smooth. Cool to lukewarm (110°-115°).

2. In a large bowl, dissolve yeast in water. Stir in milk mixture, eggs and yolk. Gradually beat in 2 cups flour. Stir in raisins, cherries and orange zest. Add enough remaining flour to form a soft dough. Turn onto a floured surface; knead dough until smooth and elastic, 6-8 minutes.

3. Place in a large greased bowl, turning once to grease top. Cover and let rise in a warm place until doubled, about 1½ hours.

4. Punch down the dough; divide into 12 portions. Shape each into a 6x4-in. oval. Place oval portions 2 in. apart on greased baking sheets.

5. For filling, crumble almond paste in a small bowl; stir in the sugar and egg white until smooth. Divide the filling into 12 portions; roll each into a 5-in. log. Flatten slightly; place off-center on each oval. Fold dough over filling; pinch edges to seal. Cover with a kitchen towel; let rise until doubled, about 45 minutes.

6. Preheat oven to 350°. Melt remaining butter; brush over each loaf. Bake until golden brown, about 20 minutes. Dust with confectioners' sugar.

1 SLICE: 121 cal., 4g fat (2g sat. fat), 16mg chol., 66mg sod., 20g carb. (9g sugars, 1g fiber), 2g pro.

ORANGE-CRANBERRY NUT BREAD

Classic flavors come together in this delicious quick bread. Orange, nuts and cranberries make this the perfect start to the morning, a tasty afternoon snack or even a sweet late-night indulgence.
—*Marilyn Ellis, Canyon Lake, PA*

Prep: 10 min.
Bake: 55 min. + cooling
Makes: 1 loaf (16 slices)

- 2 cups all-purpose flour
- 1 cup sugar
- 1½ tsp. baking powder
- ½ tsp. baking soda
- ¼ tsp. salt
- ½ cup orange juice
- 1 large egg, room temperature, lightly beaten
- 2 Tbsp. hot water
- 2 Tbsp. melted butter
- 8 oz. fresh cranberries, halved
- ½ cup chopped pecans
- 4 tsp. grated orange zest

1. Preheat oven to 325°. Whisk together the first five ingredients. In another bowl, whisk orange juice, egg, water and butter. Stir into the dry ingredients just until moistened. Fold in cranberries, pecans and orange zest.
2. Bake in a greased 9x5-in. loaf pan until a toothpick inserted in center comes out clean, 55-60 minutes. Cool 10 minutes before removing from pan to a wire rack.

1 SLICE: 155 cal., 4g fat (1g sat. fat), 15mg chol., 138mg sod., 28g carb. (14g sugars, 1g fiber), 2g pro. **DIABETIC EXCHANGES:** 2 starch, 1 fat.

> **READER RAVE**
> *"I make this every Thanksgiving and Christmas. Each time I wonder why I don't make it throughout the year. It's so good!"*
> —SHERRY, TASTEOFHOME.COM

SUGAR PLUM PHYLLO KRINGLE

Thanks to store-bought phyllo dough, this pastry comes together easily so it's perfect for gifting. It's lovely with coffee in the morning, but also for dessert with a scoop of ice cream.
—*Johnna Johnson, Scottsdale, AZ*

Prep: 30 min.
Bake: 20 min. + cooling
Makes: 6 servings

- ¾ cup chopped dried apricots
- ½ cup dried cherries
- ⅓ cup water
- ¼ cup sugar
- ¼ cup raisins
- ¾ cup chopped walnuts
- 1 Tbsp. lemon juice
- 1 pkg. (8 oz.) cream cheese, softened
- 12 sheets (14x9 in. each) phyllo dough
  Butter-flavored cooking spray
  Confectioners' sugar

1. Preheat oven to 375°. In a large saucepan, bring apricots, cherries, water, sugar and raisins to a boil. Reduce heat; simmer, uncovered, until the liquid is thickened, 6-8 minutes. Stir in walnuts and lemon juice. Remove from heat; cool mixture completely.

2. In a small bowl, beat cream cheese until smooth. Place one sheet of phyllo dough on a work surface; spritz with cooking spray. Layer with remaining phyllo, spritzing each layer. Spread cream cheese over phyllo to within 2 in. of edges; top with dried fruit mixture. Fold in edges; roll up, starting with a long side.

3. Place in a parchment-lined 15x10x1-in. baking pan, seam side down. Spritz top with cooking spray. Bake until golden brown, 20-25 minutes. Cool on a wire rack. Sprinkle with confectioners' sugar.

1 SLICE: 446 cal., 25g fat (9g sat. fat), 38mg chol., 224mg sod., 52g carb. (31g sugars, 3g fiber), 7g pro.

CHERRY CITRUS PASTRIES

Homemade candied citrus strips were the inspiration for these petite, cream cheese-rich cherry pastries. They might take a little extra time to prepare but are well worth it!
—*Lily Julow, Lawrenceville, GA*

Prep: 1 hour + chilling
Bake: 15 min. + cooling
Makes: 3 dozen

- 2 large grapefruit
- ⅔ cup water
- ⅓ cup sugar

PASTRIES
- 2 cups all-purpose flour
- 2 Tbsp. sugar
- 1 cup cold butter, cubed
- 1 pkg. (8 oz.) cream cheese, softened and cubed
- ⅓ cup cherry preserves

1. Using a vegetable peeler, peel the grapefruit making wide strips. With a sharp knife, remove white pith from peel. Cut peel into ¼-in. strips. (Save the fruit for another use.)

2. Place the grapefruit strips in a small saucepan; add water to cover. Bring to a boil. Cover and cook 10 minutes; drain.

3. In the same saucepan, combine ⅔ cup water, sugar and the grapefruit strips; bring to a boil. Reduce heat; simmer, uncovered, until peels are transparent, 12-15 minutes, stirring occasionally.

4. Using a slotted spoon, transfer strips to a wire rack placed over a baking pan. Let stand overnight. Meanwhile, in a large bowl, whisk flour and sugar. Cut in butter and cream cheese until the mixture is crumbly. Turn onto a lightly floured surface; knead gently 8-10 times.

5. Roll dough into a 12x10-in. rectangle or oval. Starting with a shorter side, fold dough into thirds, forming a 4x10-in. rectangle. Place folded dough with longer side facing you; repeat rolling and folding twice, always ending with a 4x10-in. rectangle. (If at any point the butter softens, chill after folding.) Cover folded dough; refrigerate overnight.

6. Preheat oven to 400°. On a lightly floured surface, roll dough into a 12-in. square. Cut into 2-in. squares. Place 1 in. apart on ungreased baking sheets. Press a deep indentation in center of each with the end of a wooden spoon handle. Fill each with a heaping ¼ tsp. preserves.

7. Bake until pastries are golden brown, 12-14 minutes. Top with candied peel; remove from pans to wire racks to cool.

1 PASTRY: 116 cal., 7g fat (5 sat. fat), 20mg chol., 61mg sod., 12 carb. (6g sugars, 0 fiber), 1g pro.

ALMOND GINGER COOKIES

Think outside the box when it's time to bake up a present. Each of these lovely cookies is topped with an almond slice.
—Shirley Warren, Thiensville, WI

Prep: 35 min.
Bake: 10 min./batch + cooling
Makes: about 3½ dozen

- 1 cup shortening
- ½ cup plus 3 Tbsp. sugar, divided
- ¼ cup packed brown sugar
- 1 large egg, room temperature
- 1 tsp. almond extract
- 2 cups all-purpose flour
- 1½ tsp. baking powder
- ¼ tsp. salt
- ⅓ cup crystallized ginger, finely chopped
- 2 Tbsp. sliced almonds

1. Preheat oven to 350°. Cream the shortening, ½ cup sugar and brown sugar until light and fluffy. Beat in egg and extract. In another bowl, whisk flour, baking powder and salt; gradually beat into creamed mixture. Stir in ginger.
2. Shape into 1-in. balls. Roll in remaining sugar. Place 2 in. apart on ungreased baking sheets. Flatten with the bottom of a glass dipped in sugar. Press an almond slice into center of each cookie.
3. Bake until edges are lightly browned, 9-11 minutes. Cool 2 minutes before removing to wire racks. Store in an airtight container.
1 COOKIE: 58 cal., 3g fat (1g sat. fat), 3mg chol., 20mg sod., 7g carb. (3g sugars, 0 fiber), 1g pro.

BACON WALNUT BREAD WITH HONEY BUTTER

My savory loaf is filled with blue cheese and bacon flavors but it's complemented by the sweetness of a homemade honey butter. Cut yourself a thick slice and slather on the butter—or wrap up the pair as a surprise for a friend.
—Pam Ivbuls, Elkhorn, NE

Prep: 25 min.
Bake: 40 min. + cooling
Makes: 1 loaf (16 slices) and ¾ cup honey butter

- 2 cups all-purpose flour
- 2 tsp. baking powder
- ½ tsp. baking soda
- ¼ tsp. salt
- ¼ tsp. coarsely ground pepper
- 1 cup half-and-half cream
- ¾ cup refrigerated blue cheese salad dressing
- 2 large eggs, room temperature
- 1 Tbsp. honey
- ⅔ cup coarsely chopped walnuts
- ½ cup bacon bits

HONEY BUTTER
- ¾ cup butter, softened
- 2 Tbsp. honey

1. Preheat oven to 325°. In a large bowl, whisk the first five ingredients. In another bowl, whisk cream, salad dressing, eggs and honey until blended. Add to flour mixture; stir just until moistened. Fold in walnuts and bacon bits.
2. Transfer to a greased and floured 9x5-in. loaf pan. Bake until a toothpick inserted in center of loaf comes out clean, 40-50 minutes. Cool bread in pan 10 minutes before removing to wire rack to cool completely.
3. In a small bowl, beat the honey butter ingredients together. Serve with bread.
1 SLICE PLUS ABOUT 2 TSP. HONEY BUTTER: 296 cal., 23g fat (9g sat. fat), 65mg chol., 350mg sod., 17g carb. (5g sugars, 1g fiber), 6g pro.

SWEET ALMOND TWISTS

When I give these as a gift, I tuck in a note saying that they're best served warmed!
—*Glo Devendittis, Waterford, CT*

. . . .

Prep: 25 min.
Bake: 15 min.
Makes: 32 twists

- 1 pkg. (17.3 oz.) frozen puff pastry, thawed
- 1 large egg
- 1 Tbsp. water
- ¼ cup almond cake and pastry filling
- 1 cup sliced almonds

1. Preheat oven to 400°. Unfold puff pastry sheets on a lightly floured surface; roll each sheet into a 15x10-in. rectangle.
2. In a small bowl, whisk egg and water; brush over rectangles. Spread pastry filling over one rectangle to within ¼ in. of edges; sprinkle with almonds. Top with remaining pastry, egg wash side down, pressing lightly.
3. Brush top with egg wash. Cut in half lengthwise; cut each rectangle crosswise into 16 strips. Twist each strip 2-3 times. Place 1 in. apart on baking sheets. Bake until golden brown, 12-14 minutes. Serve twists warm.

1 TWIST: 101 cal., 6g fat (1g sat. fat), 6mg chol., 56mg sod., 11g carb. (1g sugars, 1g fiber), 2g pro.

TEA BREAD

My aunt brought her tea bread recipe with her from Scotland, and enjoying a fresh-baked loaf has become a family tradition during the holidays. Each slice is loaded with red cherries.
—*Kathleen Showers, Briggsdale, CO*

. . . .

Prep: 15 min.
Bake: 1¼ hours + cooling
Makes: 2 loaves (16 slices each)

- 1 can (8 oz.) almond paste
- ¼ cup butter, softened
- 1 cup sugar
- 3 large eggs, room temperature
- 1½ cups fresh pitted cherries or blueberries
- 3 cups all-purpose flour, divided
- 4 tsp. baking powder
- ½ tsp. salt
- ¾ cup whole milk

1. In a large bowl, combine almond paste and butter; beat until well blended. Gradually add sugar, beating until light and fluffy. Add the eggs, one at a time, beating well after each addition. In a small bowl, gently toss cherries and 1 Tbsp. flour. Set aside.
2. Combine the baking powder, salt, remaining flour; add to the creamed mixture alternately with milk, beating well after each addition.
3. Spoon a sixth of the batter into each of two greased and floured 8x4-in. loaf pans; sprinkle layers with half of the fruit. Cover with another layer of batter and sprinkle with remaining fruit. Top with remaining batter; smooth with spatula.
4. Bake at 350° until a toothpick inserted in the center comes out clean, about 1¼ hours. Cool for 10 minutes before removing from pans to wire racks to cool.

1 SLICE: 130 cal., 4g fat (1g sat. fat), 25mg chol., 111mg sod., 21g carb. (10g sugars, 1g fiber), 3g pro.

> **HOMEMADE HELPER**
> Amp up your gifting game when you set a loaf of homemade bread in a brand new loaf pan. Not only will your friend enjoy the tasty surprise, but they'll think of you each time they use their new pan.

ORANGE-ALMOND CHOCLAVA

Gift-giving has never been yummier than with this chocolate twist on a classic baklava recipe.
—*Nella Parker, Hersey, MI*

Prep: 1 hour
Bake: 50 min. + chilling
Makes: about 6 dozen

- 1 lb. slivered almonds
- 1 cup semisweet chocolate chips
- ¾ cup sugar
- 2 Tbsp. grated orange zest
- 1½ cups butter, melted
- 1 pkg. (16 oz., 14x9-in. sheets) frozen phyllo dough, thawed

SYRUP
- 1¼ cups orange juice
- ¾ cup sugar
- ½ cup honey
- 2 Tbsp. lemon juice

DRIZZLE
- 2 oz. semisweet chocolate, chopped
- 3 Tbsp. water

1. Preheat oven to 325°. Place almonds and chocolate chips in a food processor; pulse until finely chopped. In a large bowl, combine almond mixture, sugar and orange zest. Brush a 15x10x1-in. baking pan with some of the butter.

2. Unroll phyllo dough. Layer 10 sheets of phyllo in prepared pan, brushing each with butter. Keep the remaining phyllo covered with a damp towel to prevent it from drying out. Sprinkle with a third of the almond mixture. Repeat layers twice. Top with remaining phyllo sheets, brushing each with butter. Cut into 1-in. diamonds. Bake until golden brown, 50-60 minutes. Meanwhile, in a saucepan, combine the syrup ingredients; bring to a boil. Reduce heat; simmer, uncovered, 20 minutes.

3. In a small heavy saucepan, heat the chocolate and water over very low heat until melted and smooth, stirring constantly. Pour the syrup over warm baklava; drizzle with chocolate mixture. Cool completely in pan on a wire rack. Refrigerate, covered, several hours or overnight. Serve at room temperature.
1 PIECE: 123 cal., 8g fat (3g sat. fat), 10mg chol., 55mg sod., 13g carb. (8g sugars, 1g fiber), 2g pro.

PISTACHIO STICKY BUNS

Looking for a fantastic contribution to a brunch buffet? Then try these ooey-gooey-good sticky buns. They rely on frozen yeast roll dough and couldn't be simpler to make. The buns rise overnight in the refrigerator, so you just need to bake them in the morning.
—*Athena Russell, Greenville, SC*

Prep: 20 min. + chilling
Bake: 30 min.
Makes: 2 dozen

- 1 cup chopped pistachios
- ½ cup dried cranberries
- 1 tsp. ground cinnamon
- 24 frozen bread dough dinner rolls, thawed
- ½ cup butter, cubed
- 1 cup packed brown sugar
- 1 pkg. (4.6 oz.) cook-and-serve vanilla pudding mix
- 2 Tbsp. 2% milk
- ½ tsp. orange extract

1. Sprinkle pistachios, cranberries and cinnamon in a greased 13x9-in. baking dish. Arrange rolls in a single layer on top.

2. In a small saucepan over low heat, melt butter. Remove from the heat; stir in the brown sugar, pudding mix, milk and extract until smooth. Pour over dough. Cover and refrigerate overnight.

3. Remove rolls from the refrigerator 30 minutes before baking. Preheat oven to 350°. Bake until rolls are golden brown, 30-35 minutes. (Cover loosely with foil if top browns too quickly.) Cool 1 minute before inverting onto a serving platter.
1 STICKY BUN: 225 cal., 8g fat (3g sat. fat), 10mg chol., 283mg sod., 36g carb. (16g sugars, 2g fiber), 5g pro.
CLASSIC STICKY BUNS: Substitute pecans and raisins for pistachios and cranberries. Omit extract.

GERMAN SOUR CREAM TWISTS

A subtle sweetness makes these pretty glazed twists just the thing for breakfast, brunch or an afternoon snack. Tie some together with ribbon for a cute gift.
—*Sally Gregg, Twinsburg, OH*

Prep: 45 min. + chilling
Bake: 15 min./batch + cooling
Makes: 2 dozen

- 1 pkg. (¼ oz.) active dry yeast
- ¼ cup warm water (110° to 115°)
- 3½ cups all-purpose flour
- 1 tsp. salt
- ⅔ cup shortening
- ⅓ cup cold butter
- 1 large egg, room temperature
- 2 large egg yolks, room temperature
- ¾ cup sour cream
- 1 tsp. vanilla extract
- 1½ cups sugar, divided
- 4 cups confectioners' sugar
- ⅓ cup half-and-half cream

1. In a small bowl, dissolve yeast in warm water. In a large bowl, combine flour and salt. Cut in shortening and butter until mixture resembles coarse crumbs. Beat in egg, egg yolks, sour cream, vanilla and yeast mixture. Cover and refrigerate for at least 2 hours. Place three ungreased baking sheets in the refrigerator.
2. Sprinkle ½ cup sugar over a clean work surface. On the sugared surface, roll half of the dough into a 12x8-in. rectangle (refrigerate remaining dough until ready to use). Sprinkle rectangle with 4 tsp. sugar; fold into thirds.
3. Give dough a quarter turn and repeat rolling, sugaring and folding two more times. Roll into a 12x8-in. rectangle. Cut into twelve 1-in.-wide strips; twist. Place on chilled baking sheets. Repeat with remaining sugar and dough.
4. Bake at 375° until lightly browned, 15-20 minutes. Immediately remove from pans to wire racks to cool.
5. For icing, combine confectioners' sugar and cream. Dip twists into icing or drizzle icing over twists.

1 TWIST: 292 cal., 10g fat (4g sat. fat), 39mg chol., 125mg sod., 47g carb. (32g sugars, 1g fiber), 3g pro.

SWEET ITALIAN HOLIDAY BREAD

This is authentic ciambellotto, a sweet loaf my great-grandmother used to bake in Italy. I use her traditional recipe but with modern appliances.
—*Denise Perrin, Vancouver, WA*

Prep: 15 min.
Bake: 45 min.
Makes: 1 loaf (20 slices)

- 4 cups all-purpose flour
- 1 cup sugar
- 2 Tbsp. grated orange zest
- 3 tsp. baking powder
- 3 large eggs, room temperature
- ½ cup 2% milk
- ½ cup olive oil
- 1 large egg yolk
- 1 Tbsp. coarse sugar

1. Preheat oven to 350°. In a large bowl, whisk flour, sugar, orange zest and baking powder. In another bowl, whisk the eggs, milk and oil until blended. Add to flour mixture; stir just until moistened.
2. Shape into a 6-in. round loaf on a greased baking sheet. Brush top with egg yolk; sprinkle with coarse sugar. Bake until a toothpick inserted in center comes out clean, 45-50 minutes. Cover top loosely with foil during last 10 minutes if needed to prevent overbrowning. Remove from pan to a wire rack; serve warm.

1 SLICE: 197 cal., 7g fat (1g sat. fat), 38mg chol., 87mg sod., 30g carb. (11g sugars, 1g fiber), 4g pro.

A GIFT FOR FIDO

Give your friend's dog a bone—and their favorite biscuits and toys—all in a tub of treats!

- Fill a large plastic tub or jar with cute colorful dog toys, biscuits and other gifts.

- Using small foam sticker letters, spell "WOOF" on a gift tag. Cut a length of ribbon to fit around the lid rim, then attach the gift tag to the ribbon using metal ball chain. Glue ribbon to the rim.

- To make a bow, cut a short length of ribbon and make a loop with ends overlapping slightly. Cut a smaller piece of ribbon, wrap it around the center of the loop and glue in back. Let dry.

- Glue the bow to the ribbon on lid. Replace the lid and stand costume reindeer antlers on top.

DOG BISCUITS

If members of your family are of the furry, four-legged kind, treat them to these homemade biscuits. They're a cinch to make, and your canine pals will go crazy for the peanut butter flavor.
—*Shannon Roum, Cudahy, WI*

Prep: 15 min.
Bake: 30 min. + cooling
Makes: 31 dog biscuits

- 2 **cups whole wheat flour**
- 1 **cup toasted wheat germ**
- ½ **tsp. ground cinnamon**
- ¾ **cup water**
- ¼ **cup creamy peanut butter**
- 1 **large egg, room temperature**
- 2 **Tbsp. canola oil**

1. Preheat oven to 350°. Combine flour, wheat germ and cinnamon. Stir in remaining ingredients. On a floured surface, roll dough to ¼-in. thickness. Cut with a 3-in. bone-shaped cookie cutter.
2. Place 2 in. apart on ungreased baking sheets. Bake until bottoms of biscuits are lightly browned (tops may crack), 30-35 minutes. Cool on a wire rack. Store in an airtight container.
NOTE: Reduced-fat peanut butter is not recommended for this recipe.
1 SERVING: 61 cal., 3g fat (0 sat. fat), 7mg chol., 12mg sod., 8g carb. (0 sugars, 1g fiber), 3g pro.

Handmade

SWEET SURPRISES

RASPBERRY NUT PINWHEELS

I won first prize in a recipe contest with these yummy swirl cookies. The taste of raspberry and walnuts really comes through each bite, and these cookies are so much fun to make!
—*Pat Habiger, Spearville, KS*

Prep: 20 min. + chilling
Bake: 10 min./batch
Makes: about 3½ dozen

- ½ cup butter, softened
- 1 cup sugar
- 1 large egg, room temperature
- 1 tsp. vanilla extract
- 2 cups all-purpose flour
- 1 tsp. baking powder
- ¼ cup seedless raspberry jam
- ¾ cup finely chopped walnuts

1. In a large bowl, cream butter and sugar until light and fluffy. Beat in the egg and vanilla. In another bowl, whisk flour and baking powder; gradually beat into the creamed mixture.
2. Roll out dough between two sheets of waxed paper into a 12-in. square. Remove waxed paper. Spread the dough with jam; sprinkle with nuts. Roll up tightly, jelly-roll style; cover. Refrigerate until firm, about 2 hours.
3. Preheat oven to 375°. Uncover dough and cut crosswise into ¼-in. slices. Place 2 in. apart on ungreased baking sheets. Bake until the edges are light brown, 9-12 minutes. Remove from pans to wire racks to cool.

1 COOKIE: 79 cal., 4g fat (1g sat. fat), 11mg chol., 27mg sod., 11g carb. (6g sugars, 0 fiber), 1g pro.

> **READER RAVE**
> *"I looooove these cookies. Cut them with dental floss to keep that nice round spiral."*
> — KIMBERLY HINES, TASTEOFHOME.COM

ALMOND PISTACHIO BAKLAVA

I discovered this traditional recipe at a Greek cultural event, and now I often get requests for it. The original version called for walnuts, but I substituted almonds and pistachios.
—*Joan Lloyd, Barrie, ON*

Prep: 1½ hours
Bake: 35 min. + standing
Makes: about 4 dozen

- 3 cups sugar, divided
- 1½ cups water
- ½ cup honey
- 5 tsp. lemon juice
- 3 cups unsalted pistachios
- 2¼ cups unsalted unblanched almonds
- 1½ tsp. ground cinnamon
- ½ tsp. ground nutmeg
- 1½ cups butter, melted
- 2 pkg. (16 oz. each, 14x9-in. sheet size) frozen phyllo dough, thawed

1. In a small saucepan, bring 2 cups sugar, water, honey and lemon juice to a boil. Reduce heat; simmer 5 minutes. Cool.
2. Preheat oven to 350°. Working in batches, combine pistachios and almonds in a food processor; cover and process until finely chopped. Transfer to a large bowl. Stir in cinnamon, nutmeg and remaining sugar; set aside. Brush a 15x10x1-in. baking pan with some of the butter. Unroll one package of phyllo dough; cut stack into a 10½x9-in. rectangle. Repeat with remaining phyllo. Discard scraps.
3. Line bottom of prepared pan with two sheets of phyllo dough (sheets will overlap slightly). Brush with butter. Repeat layers 9 times. (Keep dough covered with a damp towel until ready to use to prevent it from drying out.) Sprinkle with a third of the nut mixture.
4. Top with 10 layers of buttered phyllo dough and a third of the nut mixture; repeat layers. Top with remaining phyllo dough, buttering each layer.
5. Using a sharp knife, cut into 1½-in. diamond shapes. Bake until golden brown, 40-45 minutes. Place pan on a wire rack. Slowly pour the cooled sugar syrup over baklava. Cover baklava and let stand overnight.

1 PIECE: 273 cal., 15g fat (5g sat. fat), 17mg chol., 178mg sod., 33g carb. (19g sugars, 2g fiber), 5g pro.

SALTED PEANUT ROLLS

A gift of homemade candy is always a hit with sweet tooths. I dip these peanut rolls in chocolate, but I think they're yummy plain as well.

—*Elizabeth Hokanson, Arborg, MB*

. . . .

Prep: 1 hour + freezing
Makes: about 5 dozen

- 1 jar (7 oz.) **marshmallow creme**
- 2 to 2¼ cups **confectioners' sugar, divided**
- 1 pkg. (14 oz.) **caramels**
- 2 Tbsp. **water**
- 4 cups **salted peanuts, chopped**
- 2 cups (12 oz.) **semisweet chocolate chips**
- 2 tsp. **shortening**

1. Line two 15x10x1-in. pans with waxed paper. In a large bowl, beat marshmallow creme and 1 cup confectioners' sugar until blended. Knead in enough remaining confectioners' sugar until mixture is smooth and easy to handle.

2. Divide mixture into four portions. Roll each portion into ½-in.-thick logs. Cut crosswise into 1½-in. pieces; place on one prepared pan. Freeze until firm, about 15 minutes. Meanwhile, heat caramels and water over low heat until melted, stirring occasionally. Working with one-fourth of the logs at a time, dip in melted caramel; roll in peanuts. Place on remaining prepared pan. Repeat with the remaining logs; freeze coated logs until set.

3. In the top of a double boiler or a metal bowl over barely simmering water, melt the chocolate chips and shortening; stir until smooth. Dip bottom of rolls into melted chocolate; allow excess to drip off. Return to prepared pans. Refrigerate until set. Store rolls between layers of waxed paper in an airtight container at room temperature.

1 PIECE: 154 cal., 9g fat (3g sat. fat), 0 chol., 48mg sod., 18g carb. (15g sugars, 3g fiber), 3g pro.

APRICOT-NUT WHITE FUDGE

I wrap up small squares of this candy with ribbon and silk holly for Christmas gifts.
—*Betty Claycomb, Alverton, PA*

Prep: 15 min. + chilling
Makes: about 2½ lbs.

- 1 pkg. (8 oz.) cream cheese, softened
- 4 cups confectioners' sugar
- 12 oz. white baking chocolate, melted and cooled
- 1½ tsp. vanilla extract
- ¾ cup chopped walnuts or pecans
- ¾ cup chopped dried apricots

1. Line a 9-in. square pan with aluminum foil, letting ends extend over sides by 1 in. Coat with cooking spray; set aside. In a large bowl, beat cream cheese until fluffy. Gradually beat in confectioners' sugar. Gradually add the white chocolate. Beat in the vanilla. Fold in the chopped nuts and apricots.
2. Spread into prepared pan. Cover and refrigerate for 8 hours or overnight. Using foil, lift fudge from pan; cut into 1-in. squares.

1 PIECE: 64 cal., 3g fat (2g sat. fat), 3mg chol., 13mg sod., 10g carb. (9g sugars, 0 fiber), 0 pro.

HOMEMADE HELPER
Since it contains no cocoa solids, white chocolate technically isn't a real chocolate. It does contain cocoa butter, which gives white chocolate its rich, buttery texture. Higher-quality white chocolate contains a high percentage of cocoa butter, which makes it melt-in-your-mouth wonderful!

WAFFLE-IRON COOKIES

The recipe for these cookies is the easiest to find in my book because it's a beautiful mess. It's covered with fingerprints, flour smudges and memories from more than 30 years!
—*Judy Taylor, Quarryville, PA*

. . . .

Prep: 10 min.
Bake: 5 min./batch + cooling
Makes: 32 cookies (8 batches)

- ½ cup butter, softened
- 1 cup sugar
- 2 large eggs, room temperature
- 1 tsp. vanilla extract
- 1½ cups all-purpose flour
- 1 tsp. baking powder
- ½ tsp. salt
   Confectioners' sugar

1. In a large bowl, cream butter and sugar until light and fluffy. Beat in eggs and vanilla. In another bowl, whisk flour, baking powder and salt; gradually beat into the creamed mixture.
2. Drop dough in batches by tablespoonfuls 3-4 in. apart onto a greased preheated waffle iron. Bake until dark brown, 2-3 minutes.
3. Remove to wire racks to cool completely. Sprinkle cookies with confectioners' sugar.
1 COOKIE: 76 cal., 3g fat (2g sat. fat), 19mg chol., 79mg sod., 11g carb. (6g sugars, 0 fiber), 1g pro.

DOUBLE DELIGHTS

You get the best of both worlds with these chocolate and vanilla cookies. They're an appealing addition to any cookie tray. I usually serve them at the holidays, when they're often the first cookies to disappear, but you can have them any time of year.
—*Ruth Ann Stelfox, Raymond, AB*

. . . .

Prep: 30 min. + chilling
Bake: 10 min./batch
Makes: About 15 dozen

CHOCOLATE DOUGH

- 1 cup butter, softened
- 1½ cups sugar
- 2 large eggs, room temperature
- 2 tsp. vanilla extract
- 2 cups all-purpose flour
- ⅔ cup baking cocoa
- ¾ tsp. baking soda
- ½ tsp. salt
- 1 cup coarsely chopped pecans
- 5 oz. white baking chocolate, chopped

VANILLA DOUGH

- 1 cup butter, softened
- 1½ cups sugar
- 2 large eggs, room temperature
- 2 tsp. vanilla extract
- 2¾ cups all-purpose flour
- 2 tsp. cream of tartar
- 1 tsp. baking soda
- ½ tsp. salt
- 1 cup coarsely chopped pecans
- 4 oz. German sweet chocolate, chopped

1. For chocolate dough, in a large bowl, cream butter and sugar until light and fluffy. Beat in eggs and vanilla. Combine the flour, cocoa, baking soda and salt; gradually add to the creamed mixture and mix well. Stir in pecans and chopped white chocolate.
2. For vanilla dough, in another large bowl, cream butter and sugar until light and fluffy. Beat in eggs and vanilla. Combine the flour, cream of tartar, baking soda and salt; gradually add to creamed mixture and mix well. Stir in pecans and German chocolate. Cover and refrigerate both doughs for 2 hours.
3. Divide both doughs in half. Shape each dough portion into a 12-in. roll; cover. Refrigerate until firm, about 3 hours.
4. Uncover and cut each roll in half lengthwise. Place a chocolate half and vanilla half together, pressing to form a log; cover. Refrigerate until the dough holds together when cut, about 1 hour.
5. Using a serrated knife, cut dough into ¼-in. slices. Place 2 in. apart on greased baking sheets. Bake at 350° until cookies are set, 8-10 minutes. Remove to wire racks to cool.
2 COOKIES: 117 cal., 7g fat (3g sat. fat), 20mg chol., 95mg sod., 13g carb. (8g sugars, 1g fiber), 1g pro.

MINI S'MORES

Want to sink your teeth into s'mores all year long? Here's the answer! Just combine marshmallow creme, chocolate and graham crackers for a sweet treat whenever you want.

—Stephanie Tewell, Elizabeth, IL

Prep: 50 min. + standing
Cook: 5 min.
Makes: about 4 dozen

- 2 cups milk chocolate chips
- ½ cup heavy whipping cream
- 1 pkg. (14.4 oz.) graham crackers, quartered
- 1 cup marshmallow creme
- 2 cartons (7 oz. each) milk chocolate for dipping
- 4 oz. white candy coating, melted, optional

1. Place chocolate chips in a small bowl. In a small saucepan, bring cream just to a boil. Pour over the chocolate; stir with a whisk until smooth. Cool to room temperature or until mixture reaches a spreading consistency, about 10 minutes.

2. Spread chocolate mixture over half of the graham crackers. Spread the marshmallow creme over remaining graham crackers; place over chocolate-covered crackers, pressing to adhere.

3. Melt dipping chocolate according to package directions. Dip each s'more halfway into dipping chocolate; allow excess to drip off. Place on waxed paper-lined baking sheets; let stand until dipping chocolate is set.

4. If desired, drizzle tops with melted white candy coating; let stand until set. Store s'mores in an airtight container in the refrigerator.

1 PIECE: 145 cal., 7g fat (4g sat. fat), 5mg chol., 66mg sod., 19g carb. (13g sugars, 1g fiber), 2g pro.

> **HOMEMADE HELPER**
> Keep on whisking! At first, the chocolate and cream mixture may look separated. But don't panic: It will smooth out with plenty of whisking.

COCONUT CRANBERRY YUMMIES

When my husband came home from the grocery store with six bags of fresh cranberries, I launched a full-scale effort to creatively use them all. Bursting with tart cranberry and sweet coconut flavor, these tasty bites are my favorite result from that experience.

—Amy Alberts, Appleton, WI

Prep: 15 min.
Bake: 10 min./batch + cooling
Makes: 5 dozen

- 1 can (14 oz.) sweetened condensed milk
- 1 pkg. (14 oz.) sweetened shredded coconut
- 1 cup white baking chips
- ¼ cup ground almonds
- 1 tsp. almond extract
- 1 cup chopped fresh or frozen cranberries

1. In a large bowl, combine the first five ingredients; mix well. Stir in cranberries. Drop by tablespoonfuls 3 in. apart onto parchment-lined baking sheets; gently shape into mounds.
2. Bake at 325° until edges are lightly browned, 10-12 minutes. Cool for 3 minutes before removing from pans to wire racks to cool completely.

1 COOKIE: 74 cal., 4g fat (3g sat. fat), 3mg chol., 28mg sod., 9g carb. (8g sugars, 0 fiber), 1g pro. **DIABETIC EXCHANGES:** ½ starch, ½ fat.

PUMPKIN-GINGERBREAD THUMBPRINT COOKIES

These cookies are the result of a recipe inspiration and an afternoon spent experimenting in the kitchen with my daughters. I took the cookies to a meeting and they were an immediate hit. So yummy with a cup of coffee!

—Jennifer Needham, Woodstock, GA

Prep: 20 min.
Bake: 10 min./batch + cooling
Makes: about 4½ dozen

- 1 pkg. (14½ oz.) gingerbread cake/cookie mix
- ¼ cup hot water
- 2 Tbsp. unsalted butter, melted
- 1 cup solid-pack pumpkin
- 1 cup all-purpose flour
- 2 to 3 tsp. pumpkin pie spice
- 54 milk chocolate kisses

1. Preheat oven to 375°. In a large bowl, combine cookie mix, hot water and butter. Stir in pumpkin. In a small bowl, whisk flour and pie spice; gradually stir into mixture. Shape dough into 1-in. balls.
2. Place 2 in. apart on ungreased baking sheets. Press a deep indentation in center of each ball with your thumb. Bake until set, 6-8 minutes. Immediately press a chocolate kiss into center of each cookie. Remove from pans to wire racks to cool.

1 COOKIE: 66 cal., 3g fat (1g sat. fat), 2mg chol., 51mg sod., 10g carb. (6g sugars, 0 fiber), 1g pro.

> **HOMEMADE HELPER**
> If you don't have pumpkin pie spice, you can make your own with a blend of 2 tsp. cinnamon, 1 tsp. ginger, and ½ tsp. each of ground nutmeg and cloves or allspice. Use in recipes that call for the spice blend.

JUMBO BROWNIE COOKIES

Bring these incredibly fudgy cookies to a party, and you're sure to make a friend. A little espresso powder in the dough makes them over-the-top good.
—*Rebecca Cababa, Las Vegas, NV*

Prep: 20 min.
Bake: 15 min./batch
Makes: about 1½ dozen

- 2⅔ cups (16 oz.) 60% cacao bittersweet chocolate baking chips
- ½ cup unsalted butter, cubed
- 4 large eggs, room temperature
- 1½ cups sugar
- 4 tsp. vanilla extract
- 2 tsp. instant espresso powder, optional
- ⅔ cup all-purpose flour
- ½ tsp. baking powder
- ¼ tsp. salt
- 1 pkg. (11½ oz.) semisweet chocolate chunks

1. Preheat oven to 350°. In a large saucepan, melt chocolate chips and butter over low heat, stirring until smooth. Remove from the heat; cool until mixture is warm.

2. In a small bowl, whisk the eggs, sugar, vanilla and, if desired, espresso powder until blended. Whisk into chocolate mixture. In another bowl, mix the flour, baking powder and salt; add to chocolate mixture, mixing well. Fold in chocolate chunks; let stand until mixture thickens slightly, about 10 minutes.

3. Drop by ¼ cupfuls 3 in. apart onto parchment-lined baking sheets. Bake until set, 12-14 minutes. Cool cookies on pans 1-2 minutes. Remove to wire racks to cool.

NOTE: This recipe was tested with Ghirardelli 60% Cacao Bittersweet Chocolate Baking Chips; results may vary when using a different product.

1 COOKIE: 350 cal., 19g fat (11g sat. fat), 60mg chol., 65mg sod., 48g carb. (40g sugars, 3g fiber), 4g pro.

CRISP BUTTER COOKIES

With just six everyday ingredients plus colored sugar, you can bake dozens of from-scratch cutouts. Arrange the crisp goodies onto a plate for your next holiday get-together.
—*Tammy Mackie, Seward, NE*

Prep: 20 min.
Bake: 10 min./batch
Makes: 2½ dozen

- ½ cup butter, softened
- 1 cup sugar
- 5 large egg yolks, room temperature
- 1½ tsp. vanilla extract
- 2 cups all-purpose flour
- ⅛ tsp. salt
  Colored sugar

1. In a large bowl, cream butter and sugar until light and fluffy. Beat in egg yolks and vanilla. In a small bowl, combine flour and salt; gradually beat into creamed mixture, mixing well (dough will be very stiff).

2. On a well-floured surface, roll out dough to ⅛-in. thickness. With a sharp knife or pastry wheel, cut dough into 2½-in. squares, rectangles or diamonds. Place 1 in. apart on ungreased baking sheets. Sprinkle with colored sugar.

3. Bake at 375° until lightly browned, 7-8 minutes. (Watch carefully as cookies will brown quickly.) Remove to wire racks to cool. Store in airtight containers.

1 COOKIE: 77 cal., 3g fat (2g sat. fat), 36mg chol., 27mg sod., 11g carb. (6g sugars, 0 fiber), 1g pro.

VALENTINE'S DAY TREAT BOXES

Transform mini popcorn boxes into adorable Valentine's Day treat-holders. Fill them with a single homemade candy to give to someone special. Or set out the empty treat boxes on your dessert table and let guests fill their own from your lineup of sweet treats.

MATERIALS

Miniature white or striped popcorn boxes
Red or pink decorative scrapbook paper or card stock
Red or pink ribbon
Heart paper punch or heart template
Craft knife
Hot glue gun
Decorative shredded paper filler, optional
Desired wrapped treats

DIRECTIONS

1. If using white boxes, trace a folded box twice onto the same scrapbook paper or card stock. Repeat for each remaining white box. Cut out pieces. Glue matching pieces to the front and back of each white box. Let dry.
2. With the template or paper punch, make a heart for each box using contrasting paper or card stock.
3. Using craft knife, cut two small slits about 1¼ in. apart in center of each heart, making the slits long enough so that the desired ribbon can be threaded through the slits.
4. For each box, cut a 16- to 24-in. length of contrasting ribbon.
5. Wrap a ribbon piece once around desired box, then thread each ribbon end from back to front through a slit on desired heart. Tie ribbon ends on front of heart as desired, securing heart on box.
6. Fill boxes with decorative shredded paper if desired. Add desired treats to each box.

CREAMY ORANGE CARAMELS

Every year I teach myself a new candy recipe. Last year I started with my caramel recipe and added a splash of orange extract for fun. This year I just might try buttered rum extract.
—*Shelly Bevington, Hermiston, OR*

Prep: 10 min.
Cook: 30 min. + standing
Makes: about 2½ lbs. (80 pieces)

- 1 tsp. plus 1 cup butter, divided
- 2 cups sugar
- 1 cup light corn syrup
- 1 can (14 oz.) sweetened condensed milk
- 1 tsp. orange extract
- 1 tsp. vanilla extract

1. Line an 11x7-in. dish with foil, letting ends extend over sides by 1 in.; grease foil with 1 tsp. butter.
2. In a large heavy saucepan, combine the sugar, corn syrup and remaining butter. Bring to a boil over medium heat, stirring constantly. Reduce the heat to medium-low; boil gently, without stirring, for 4 minutes.
3. Remove from the heat; gradually stir in the milk. Cook and stir until a candy thermometer reads 244° (firm-ball stage). Remove from the heat; stir in extracts. Immediately pour into prepared dish (do not scrape saucepan). Let stand until firm.
4. Using foil, lift out candy; remove foil. Using a buttered knife, cut caramel into scant 1½x1-in. pieces. Wrap individually in waxed paper; twist ends.

NOTE: We recommend that you test your candy thermometer before each use by bringing water to a boil; the thermometer should read 212°. Adjust your recipe temperature up or down based on your test.

1 PIECE: 69 cal., 3g fat (2g sat. fat), 8mg chol., 27mg sod., 11g carb. (11g sugars, 0 fiber), 0 pro.

HOMEMADE MANGO MARSHMALLOWS

Homemade marshmallows are much better than bagged ones. I had yummy results when I flavored my recipe with mango nectar. Look for it in your store's Hispanic food section.

—*Deirdre Cox, Kansas City, MO*

. . . .

Prep: 25 min.
Cook: 20 min. + cooling
Makes: 1½ lbs.

  2   **envelopes unflavored gelatin**
1¼   **cups chilled mango**
      nectar, divided
1½   **cups sugar**
  ¾   **cup light corn syrup**
  1   **tsp. almond extract**
  2   **cups sweetened shredded**
      coconut, toasted

1. Line an 8-in. square pan with foil, letting ends extend over sides by 1 in.; grease the foil with cooking spray. In a heatproof bowl of a stand mixer, sprinkle gelatin over ½ cup nectar.

2. In a large heavy saucepan, combine sugar, corn syrup and remaining nectar. Bring to a boil, stirring occasionally. Cook mixture, without stirring, over medium heat until a candy thermometer reads 240° (soft-ball stage).

3. Remove from heat; slowly drizzle into gelatin, beating on high speed. Continue beating until very stiff and doubled in volume, about 10 minutes. Immediately beat in extract. Spread into prepared pan. Cover and let cool at room temperature 6 hours or overnight.

4. Place coconut in a food processor; process until finely chopped. Using foil, lift the candy out of pan. Using lightly buttered kitchen scissors, cut into 1-in. pieces. Roll in the coconut. Store in an airtight container in a cool, dry place.

NOTE: To toast coconut, bake in a shallow pan in a 350° oven for 5-10 minutes or cook in a skillet over low heat until golden brown, stirring occasionally.

1 MARSHMALLOW: 48 cal., 1g fat (1g sat. fat), 0 chol., 11mg sod., 10g carb. (10g sugars, 0 fiber), 0 pro.

Handmade
HOLIDAY FAVORITES

TINY TIM SANDWICH COOKIES

When I was growing up, my mother and I created special Christmas memories in the kitchen preparing these adorable bite-sized cookies. Vary the food coloring for holidays throughout the year.
—*Eudora Delezenne, Port Huron, MI*

Prep: 45 min.
Bake: 10 min./batch + cooling
Makes: about 5 dozen

- 1 cup sugar, divided
- 2 to 3 drops red food coloring
- 2 to 3 drops green food coloring
- ½ cup butter, softened
- ½ cup shortening
- ¼ cup confectioners' sugar
- 1 tsp. almond extract
- 2⅓ cups all-purpose flour

FROSTING
- 2 cups confectioners' sugar
- 3 Tbsp. butter, softened
- 4½ tsp. heavy whipping cream
- ¾ tsp. almond extract
  Red and green food coloring, optional

1. Preheat oven to 375°. Combine ½ cup sugar and red food coloring; set aside. In another bowl, combine remaining sugar with green food coloring; set aside.
2. In a large bowl, cream the butter, shortening and confectioners' sugar until light and fluffy. Beat in extract. Gradually beat in flour. Shape into ½-in. balls.
3. Place 1 in. apart on ungreased baking sheets. Coat bottoms of two glasses with cooking spray, then dip one in red sugar and the other in green sugar. Flatten cookies alternately with prepared glasses, redipping in sugar as needed. Bake until edges are lightly browned, 8-10 minutes. Remove to wire racks to cool completely.
4. For frosting, combine confectioners' sugar, butter, cream and extract. If desired, use food coloring to tint half of the frosting red and the other half green. Frost the bottoms of half of the cookies; cover with remaining cookies.

1 SANDWICH COOKIE: 83 cal., 4g fat (2g sat. fat), 6mg chol., 17mg sod., 12g carb. (8g sugars, 0 fiber), 1g pro.

CHIVE BISCUIT ORNAMENTS

Ring in the holiday season with a basket of these tender star-shaped bites. They are a fun, change-of-pace hostess gift!
—*Taste of Home Test Kitchen*

Takes: 30 min.
Makes: 1 dozen

- 3¼ cups biscuit/baking mix
- ½ cup shredded cheddar cheese
- 1 Tbsp. minced chives
- 1 tsp. crushed red pepper flakes
- 1 cup heavy whipping cream
- 12 whole chives

1. In a large bowl, combine the biscuit mix, cheese, minced chives and pepper flakes. Stir in cream just until moistened.
2. Turn onto a lightly floured surface; knead 8-10 times. Pat to ½-in. thickness. Cut with a floured 3-in. star-shaped cookie cutter. Using a ½-in. round cookie cutter, cut a hole near top of each biscuit.
3. Place 2 in. apart on ungreased baking sheets. Bake at 450° until golden brown, 8-10 minutes. Remove to wire racks. Thread one whole chive through each biscuit hole; tie a knot. Serve warm.

1 BISCUIT: 218 cal., 14g fat (7g sat. fat), 32mg chol., 445mg sod., 21g carb. (1g sugars, 1g fiber), 4g pro.

> **HOMEMADE HELPER**
> These biscuits hold their shape relatively well, so feel free to use cookie cutters shaped like bells, trees or stockings when preparing the savory delights.

CHRISTMAS CRANBERRIES

Bourbon adds bite to this yuletide treat. Wrap a jar in a tea towel or cloth napkin, cinch with ribbon and adorn with a small ornament for gift-giving.

—*Becky Jo Smith, Kettle Falls, WA*

. . . .

Prep: 35 min.
Process: 15 min.
Makes: 4 half-pints

- 2 pkg. (12 oz. each) fresh or frozen cranberries, thawed
- 1½ cups sugar
- 1 cup orange juice
- ¼ cup bourbon
- 3 tsp. vanilla extract
- 1 tsp. grated orange zest

1. In a large saucepan, combine cranberries, sugar, orange juice and bourbon. Bring to a boil. Reduce heat; simmer, uncovered, until the cranberries pop and the mixture has thickened, 18-22 minutes.

2. Remove from heat. Stir in vanilla and orange zest. Ladle hot mixture into four hot half-pint jars, leaving ¼-in. headspace. Remove the air bubbles and adjust headspace, if necessary, by adding hot mixture. Wipe rims. Center lids on jars; screw on bands until fingertip tight.

3. Place jars into canner with simmering water, ensuring that they are completely covered with water. Bring to a boil; process for 15 minutes. Remove the jars and cool.

NOTE: The processing time listed is for altitudes of 1,000 feet or less. Add 1 minute to the processing time for each 1,000 feet of additional altitude.

2 TBSP.: 54 cal., 0 fat (0 sat. fat), 0 chol., 0 sod., 13g carb. (11g sugars, 1g fiber), 0 pro.

WHITE FRUITCAKE

Years ago, when I attended a missionary church in Hawaii, a friend gave me this recipe. Now I whip up at least 60 loaves for holiday presents.
—*Eileen Flatt, Chandler, AZ*

. . . .

Prep: 20 min.
Bake: 50 min. + cooling
Makes: 4 loaves (16 slices each)

- 1 pkg. (8 oz.) chopped mixed candied fruit
- 1¼ cups golden raisins
- 1 cup chopped walnuts, toasted
- 3 cups all-purpose flour, divided
- 2 cups butter, softened
- 2 cups sugar
- 6 large eggs, room temperature

1. Preheat oven to 275°. Line bottoms of four greased 9x5-in. loaf pans with parchment; grease parchment.
2. In a small bowl, toss candied fruit, raisins and walnuts with ½ cup flour.
3. In a large bowl, cream butter and sugar until light and fluffy. Add eggs, one at a time, beating well after each addition. Gradually beat in remaining flour. Fold in fruit mixture.
4. Transfer to prepared pans. Bake until a toothpick inserted in center comes out clean, 50-60 minutes. Cool in pans for 10 minutes before removing to wire racks to cool.

NOTE: To toast nuts, bake in a shallow pan in a 350° oven for 5-10 minutes or cook in a skillet over low heat until lightly browned, stirring occasionally.

1 SLICE: 133 cal., 7g fat (4g sat. fat), 33mg chol., 61mg sod., 16g carb. (10g sugars, 1g fiber), 2g pro.

> **READER RAVE**
> *"This is a great recipe, I make it in small aluminum loaf pans to give as gifts. Yummy!"*
> —KITTYKAT12, TASTEOFHOME.COM

CHRISTMAS HARD CANDY

My mom always makes this candy, and people request it every year. She puts it in clear jars with a holiday calico fabric on the lid. Now I've started making it, too. When I prepare a batch of this beautiful jewel-toned candy, the whole house fills with wonderful aromas.

—Jane Holman, Moultrie, GA

. . . .

Prep: 5 min.
Cook: 1 hour + cooling
Makes: about 2 lbs.

- 3½ cups sugar
- 1 cup light corn syrup
- 1 cup water
- ¼ to ½ tsp. cinnamon or peppermint oil
- 1 tsp. red or green food coloring

1. In a large heavy saucepan, combine the sugar, corn syrup and water. Cook on medium-high heat until a candy thermometer reads 300° (hard-crack stage), stirring occasionally. Remove from the heat; stir in the oil and food coloring, keeping face away from mixture as aroma is very strong.

2. Immediately pour onto an oiled baking sheet. Cool; break into pieces. Store in airtight containers.

NOTE: Cinnamon oil and peppermint oil are available in cake decorating and candy supply stores.

1 PIECE: 114 cal., 0 fat (0 sat. fat), 0 chol., 13mg sod., 30g carb. (26g sugars, 0 fiber), 0 pro.

OVERNIGHT REINDEER ROLLS

Have some family fun making these cute reindeer-shaped rolls with the kids. Make sure to take pictures of the final product because the rolls will be gone before you know it!

—Chris O'Connell, San Antonio, TX

. . . .

Prep: 50 min. + rising
Bake: 10 min.
Makes: 3 dozen

- 2 pkg. (¼ oz. each) active dry yeast
- 1½ cups warm water (110° to 115°)
- 2 large eggs, room temperature
- ½ cup butter, softened
- ½ cup sugar
- 2 tsp. salt
- 5¾ to 6¼ cups all-purpose flour
  DECORATIONS
- 1 large egg
- 2 tsp. water
- 36 raisins (about 2 Tbsp.), halved
- 18 red candied cherries, halved

1. In a small bowl, dissolve yeast in warm water. In a large bowl, combine the eggs, butter, sugar, salt, yeast mixture and 3 cups flour; beat on medium speed until smooth. Stir in enough remaining flour to form a very soft dough (dough will be sticky). Do not knead. Cover and refrigerate overnight.

2. Turn dough onto a floured surface; divide and shape into 36 balls. Roll each into a 5-in. log. Cut each log lengthwise halfway down the center. Pull the cut sections apart for antlers. Using kitchen shears, snip ½-in. cuts along outer sides for antler points. Flatten uncut half of log for face.

3. Place 2 in. apart on greased baking sheets. Cover with kitchen towels; let rise in a warm place until doubled, about 30 minutes. Preheat oven to 400°.

4. In a small bowl, whisk egg and water until blended; brush over the rolls. Press raisin halves into dough for the eyes; press cherry halves into dough for noses. Bake until golden brown, 8-10 minutes. Serve warm.

1 ROLL: 116 cal., 3g fat (2g sat. fat), 24mg chol., 155mg sod., 19g carb. (5g sugars, 1g fiber), 3g pro.

FRUITCAKE CHRISTMAS COOKIES

My rich fruit- and nut-filled drop cookies are a deliciously fun take on traditional fruitcake. They make great gifts for folks who love the old-fashioned treat. Their flavor actually gets better over time!

—*Julia Funkhouser, Carson, IA*

Prep: 25 min.
Bake: 15 min./batch
Makes: about 3½ dozen

- 1 cup butter, softened
- ¾ cup packed brown sugar
- 1 large egg, room temperature
- ½ tsp. vanilla extract
- 1⅔ cups all-purpose flour
- ½ tsp. baking soda
- ¼ tsp. salt
- 1½ cups dates, finely chopped
- 4 oz. red candied cherries, halved
- 4 oz. candied pineapple, diced
- ½ cup whole hazelnuts, toasted
- ½ cup coarsely chopped pecans
- ½ cup coarsely chopped walnuts

1. Preheat oven to 325°. In a large bowl, cream butter and brown sugar until light and fluffy. Beat in the egg and vanilla. In another bowl, whisk together the flour, baking soda and salt; gradually beat into creamed mixture. Stir in remaining ingredients.

2. Drop dough by teaspoonfuls onto greased baking sheets. Bake until golden brown, about 15 minutes. Store in an airtight container.

NOTE: To toast whole hazelnuts, bake in a shallow pan in a 350° oven until fragrant and lightly browned, 7-10 minutes, stirring occasionally. To remove skins, wrap the hazelnuts in a tea towel; rub with towel to loosen skins.

1 COOKIE: 265 cal., 15g fat (6g sat. fat), 33mg chol., 168mg sod., 33g carb. (23g sugars, 2g fiber), 3g pro.

CANDY CANE CHOCOLATE LOAVES

When I had a bunch of leftover candy canes after the holidays, I was inspired to add them to a chocolate bread. Coffee and cocoa intensify the overall flavor.

—*Shelly Platten, Amherst, WI*

Prep: 25 min.
Bake: 50 min. + cooling
Makes: 3 loaves (12 slices each)

- ¼ cup butter, softened
- 1⅔ cups packed brown sugar
- 4 large egg whites, room temperature

- 2 large eggs, room temperature
- ¾ cup strong brewed coffee
- ½ cup vanilla yogurt
- ¼ cup canola oil
- 1 Tbsp. vanilla extract
- ¼ tsp. peppermint extract
- 3½ cups all-purpose flour
- ¾ cup baking cocoa
- 1½ tsp. baking soda
- ½ tsp. salt
- 1½ cups buttermilk
- 1 cup (6 oz.) miniature semisweet chocolate chips

TOPPING
- 2 oz. white baking chocolate, melted
- 3 Tbsp. crushed candy canes

1. Preheat oven to 350°. Coat three 8x4-in. loaf pans with cooking spray. In a large bowl, beat butter and brown sugar until crumbly, about 2 minutes. Add egg whites, eggs, coffee, yogurt, oil and extracts until blended.

2. In another bowl, whisk flour, cocoa, baking soda and salt; add to brown sugar mixture alternately with buttermilk, beating well after each addition. Fold in chocolate chips.

3. Transfer to prepared pans. Bake until a toothpick inserted in center comes out clean, 50-55 minutes. Cool 10 minutes before removing from pans to wire racks to cool completely.

4. Drizzle the melted white baking chocolate over loaves. Sprinkle with the crushed candies.

1 SLICE: 162 cal., 5g fat (2g sat. fat), 16mg chol., 124mg sod., 26g carb. (15g sugars, 1g fiber), 3g pro.

HOLIDAY EGGNOG MIX

Eggnog fans will be thrilled to receive this convenient mix. It lasts up to 6 months, so creamy glassfuls can keep on coming throughout the winter season.

—*Melissa Hansen, Ellison Bay, WI*

Takes: 10 min.
Makes: 18 servings (6 cups eggnog mix)

- 6⅔ **cups nonfat dry milk powder**
- 2 **pkg. (3.4 oz. each) instant vanilla pudding mix**
- 1 **cup buttermilk blend powder**
- 1 **Tbsp. ground nutmeg**

ADDITIONAL INGREDIENT
(FOR EACH BATCH)
- ¾ **cup cold whole milk**

1. In a food processor, combine the first four ingredients; cover and pulse until blended. Store in airtight containers in a cool, dry place for up to 6 months.
2. To prepare eggnog: Place ⅓ cup mix in a glass. Stir in ¾ cup milk until blended.

¾ CUP PREPARED EGGNOG: 267 cal., 7g fat (4g sat. fat), 27mg chol., 398mg sod., 35g carb. (33g sugars, 0 fiber), 17g pro.

DOUBLE CHOCOLATE WALNUT FUDGE

Anyone who's fond of chocolate will fall in love with this smooth, nutty fudge two times over. I enjoy making several batches when Christmas rolls around. It doesn't last long at our house during the merry December festivities!

—*Florence Hasty, Louisiana, MO*

Prep: 10 min.
Cook: 20 min. + chilling
Makes: about 2½ lbs. (81 servings)

- 1 **tsp. butter**
- 1 **pkg. (12 oz.) semisweet chocolate chips**
- 1 **can (14 oz.) sweetened condensed milk, divided**
- 1 **cup chopped walnuts, divided**
- 2 **tsp. vanilla extract, divided**
- 1 **pkg. (11½ oz.) milk chocolate chips**

1. Line a 9-in. square pan with foil, letting ends extend over sides by 1 in.; grease foil with butter.
2. In a large heavy saucepan, combine semisweet chocolate chips and ¾ cup milk over low heat. Remove from heat; stir in ½ cup walnuts and 1 tsp. vanilla. Spread into prepared pan.
3. In another saucepan, combine milk chocolate chips and remaining milk. Remove from heat; stir in remaining walnuts and vanilla. Spread over first layer. Refrigerate, covered, until firm, about 2 hours. Using foil, lift fudge out of pan. Remove foil; cut fudge into 1-in. squares. Store between layers of waxed paper in an airtight container.

1 PIECE: 69 cal., 4g fat (2g sat. fat), 3mg chol., 10mg sod., 8g carb. (7g sugars, 0 fiber), 1g pro.

• • •

CHOCOLATE SNOWBALLS

This is my all-time favorite Christmas cookie recipe. They are so easy and loaded with flavor. The treats remind me of the snowballs I'd pack as a child during frosty winter days in Wisconsin.
—*Dee Derezinski, Waukesha, WI*

Prep: 30 min.
Bake: 15 min./batch + cooling
Makes: about 4 dozen

- ¾ cup butter, softened
- ½ cup sugar
- ½ tsp. salt
- 1 large egg, room temperature
- 2 tsp. vanilla extract
- 2 cups all-purpose flour
- 1 cup chopped pecans or walnuts
- 1 cup (6 oz.) chocolate chips
  Confectioners' sugar

1. Preheat oven to 350°. In a large bowl, cream butter, sugar and salt until light and fluffy. Beat in egg and vanilla. Gradually beat in flour. Stir in pecans and chocolate chips.
2. Shape dough into 1-in. balls; place 2 in. apart on ungreased baking sheets. Bake until set and bottoms are lightly browned, 15-20 minutes. Cool on pans 2 minutes. Gently roll the warm cookies in the confectioners' sugar. Cool completely on wire racks. If desired, reroll cookies in confectioners' sugar.

1 COOKIE: 92 cal., 6g fat (3g sat. fat), 12mg chol., 49mg sod., 10g carb. (5g sugars, 1g fiber), 1g pro.

> **READER RAVE**
> *"Discovered this recipe last year and it's fantastic. The best snowball recipe ever! We love all of the chocolate chips in them."*
> —SUSANRUKES, TASTEOFHOME.COM

SNOWMAN JAR

Transform an old jar into a frosty friend filled with snowy white cookies or candies—a perfect treat for someone sweet!

MATERIALS
Mason jar
Black craft foam
Black spray paint
2 fabric strips: 1 short, 1 longer
3 black buttons

DIRECTIONS
1. Coat the lid and outside band of a large canning jar with black spray paint. Let dry.
2. Place the jar upside down on a piece of black craft foam; trace around the mouth of the jar. Draw a second circle 1 in. larger around the traced circle. Cut along the outside circle, then cut along the inner circle to form a ring.
3. Wrap the long fabric strip around the top of the jar; cross the ends to make a scarf. Wrap the small fabric strip around the point where the ends cross; glue the small strip at the back.
4. Glue black buttons down front of the jar. Let dry.
5. Slip the foam ring over the top of the jar. Fill the jar with treats and screw on the lid.

RECIPE, CRAFT & GIFT INDEX